D1588346

Lakeland Gamekeeper

LAKELAND GAMEKEEPER

LAKELAND
GAMEKEEPER

David Imrie

LONDON
THE BATCHWORTH PRESS

PUBLISHED IN 1949 BY
BATCHWORTH PRESS LTD
20 TUDOR STREET, EC4

PRINTED IN GREAT BRITAIN BY
JAMES UPTON LTD
LONDON AND BIRMINGHAM

Contents

Illustrations

Foreword .

THIS is a book for shooting men and other people of the open air who have had experience of, or at least some sympathy with, a phase of country life which appears to be passing.

It is the summary of a gamekeeper's everyday experiences in the Lake District over a period of some twenty years, and was written by a man who has lived for the whole of that time (except for occasional visits to the Yorkshire moors) in a wooden, fellside hut at the entrance to Newlands Valley.

When he came to the Lake District, gamekeepers were numerous. Gradually, however, they dwindled away, and now the Author of this book is the sole representative of a vanished race.

Many a man compelled, as David Imrie has been, to spend much of his time alone would have turned into a recluse, or taken to drink. He has done neither. People, the world's affairs, his love of Nature, his hobbies, and his interesting job have combined to keep him comparatively sane.

His job, by the way, is not quite what it used to be. Formerly he reared game by hand, and was more truly a gamekeeper than he is now. The war accelerated that change. He is of the opinion that the change is permanent.

Nowadays the Author is mainly a vermin destroyer in the interests of agriculture. If game happens to benefit thereby, well and good, but agriculture comes first.

Let no one think, however, that he is an indiscriminate destroyer. After years of close observation he has revised his ideas on the vermin question, and has come to the conclusion that the only two genuine nuisances in the Lake

District are the fox and carrion crow. Unlike many other creatures that come under the category of 'pests' they have no redeeming features.

But this book is more than a record of gamekeeping incidents. It is partly biography, written by a poet ; for David Imrie has been known for many years as the gamekeeper's poet and his work is well-known to the readers of several sporting periodicals.

When the last page of this book is reached, one may have formed some idea of the Author's personality.

I. COUNTRY

The Hut and Surroundings   *The Estate*

Derwent Bog

THIS hut, which has been for twenty years my home, stands in a woodland glade on the north shoulder of Barrow Fell at the entrance to Newlands Valley.

I have been told that it had only one room originally, and was heated by a closed stove ; but that was before my day. Ever since I knew the hut it has had two rooms and an open, coal-burning fireplace. The kitchen is part of an army hut of 1914 vintage. If I had been present at the sawing operation, I might have made that original part slightly bigger. It is only ten feet wide by eighteen long. In it are two windows. The side window, looking to the east, gives me a restricted view of glossy, dark-green, Scots fir foliage, but the bigger front window frames a glorious picture of Derwent Bog and Lake Bassenthwaite.

The bedroom is even smaller than the kitchen. Its floor is practically square, about ten feet each way. The one window looks across fifty yards of green-sward and bracken to the main part of the wood, which rises steeply. If I stand upright in the bedroom, I see grass, bracken and trees ; but when I lie in bed, the sky and some oak trees at the summit of the wood are visible. And that summit is, by the way, a little plateau detached from the main fell. Often on early, summer mornings I have lain and watched pigeons and magpies settle in those oaks. The furnishings of the bedroom are spartan in their simplicity : a bed, a trunk, some suit-cases, a set of bagpipes, a leather gun-case, which holds a beautiful, old, Damascus-barrelled gun, and a couple of coats on one wall. There are no chairs in the bedroom ; so I sit on the edge of the bed when I wish to

9

read or write on a softer seat than the kitchen chairs provide.

The bedroom walls, and the walls of the kitchen also, are covered halfway up with dark, varnished boarding. The upper half is stout beaver boarding, distempered light green. The ceiling and rafters are white-washed, but I daresay that another coat of white-wash would make them even whiter than they are now. On the floor there is no covering at all.

It is not so easy to describe the kitchen ; so a summary will have to suffice. Books are conspicuous. The one shelf along the back wall supports a row of books on widely different subjects, and there are books on the dresser under the side window. Those books come and go. If I kept all the books I read, the hut would now be like a library.

In the corner by the dresser are several shotguns and two powerful air rifles. The latter are useful for destroying young rabbits. They are both .22 bore. My gamebag is often lying over by that dresser also.

The fireplace is exactly opposite the front window. It isn't very elegant, but it does the turn. If I pull the damper, the oven heats as quickly as anyone could wish. There are three chairs standing about on the bareboarded floor, and another, a bed-chair, tucked in the corner under my cupboard, which is on the wall at the left of the window. The table under the front window is covered with a clean, white tablecloth at the moment. At other times the tablecloth is patterned. A fresh one is put on every fortnight. My artificial light is provided by a Tilley pressure lamp, which stands permanently on the table. Every time I come up the path to the hut I see the white shade through the window. The mantelpiece is a repository for various small items ; cartridges in their cartons and the tea-caddy are the most important of these.

There is no water-tap in the hut, nor is there one near it. I get my drinking water from a miniature waterfall along the wood. It gushes out of the rock a dozen yards above where I draw my supply, and no water could be purer. A sheep did once decide to die near the source, but luckily I spotted the carcase in time. The spring is shaded by spruces and tall laurels ; so I could easily have missed it. One day I counted the paces I took between the hut and the waterfall. They came to six hundred and fifty.

For other domestic uses except cooking I use rainwater. It is collected in a tank at the front from the longer slope of the hut roof, and only fails me in a very great drought. During the summer, however, I have often been compelled to empty it on account of the green scum which is apt to form on all stagnant water then. Never have I drunk it, but I daresay after a heavy rain it would be quite good.

The outside walls of the hut are tarred. The door is painted green, and the roof is felted and tarred. In summer the thinness of the roof causes the hut to be very warm sometimes ; in winter it is often cold for the same reason. But I have usually had plenty of fuel ; so I can combat anything but excessive cold. A north wind is worst, because that is the unprotected side ; and if a north wind combines with a low temperature, I have to stoke up very hard, indeed.

Although this is a flimsy abode, I have only once feared for its safety. That was about four years ago. A furious gale blew up one night. It went from the west to the north and grew worse. I was alarmed. The old place shook violently, and I felt that a little more pressure would blow it asunder, but the night got past without mishap. Then about eight o'clock in the morning the chimney pot went with a wallop on the roof. Immediately, the hut was filled with smoke and soot. The shortened, jagged remains of the pot caught the wind. I had just to suffer in silence. Finally, I put out the fire gradually with a bucket of water. That abated the smoke nuisance and the danger of fire, but the place was anything but comfortable. Every savage gust brought down more soot. However, I went off on my usual trek, hoping that the hut would be intact when I returned.

About midday I came back, lit the fire and had dinner. The smoke nuisance then was not quite so bad, for some obscure reason ; so when I had finished dinner, I rose to go outside for a shovelful of coal. I barely got to the door when a fearful gust struck the hut. The door burst open, and before I could shut it, there was a tremendous crack. The end wall was blown clear of the floor. I jumped outside, and pulled the door behind me, otherwise the whole structure would have gone like a bundle of newspapers. But the door refused to catch. I hung on grimly, and at the first lull, I tied the door-handle with string to a nail in the wall. My labrador bitch, Peggy, was inside when the crack occurred. She got a terrible fright, and I saw her wriggle out through the gap between the floor and the wall. I got a fright, too. When the door was secure, I pushed back the wall into its proper position with a fencing post, which happened to be lying handy. Then I drove the post into the ground to avoid a repetition of the disaster. A few days later the estate joiner made the wall secure, and it has remained secure ever since, but I still hate a north wind.

But I have had more pleasant times in the hut than bad ones. I can hear the birds sing in the nearby trees even when the door is shut, and the sough of the wind on a winter night is a lullaby. As a building it is more in harmony with its surroundings than a stone-built structure. And I can pass a happy evening before the fire with a book. Some time between nine and ten I will make myself a cup of tea, then another short session of reading, and into bed, at peace with all the world.

The glade in which the hut stands is perhaps a hundred and fifty yards long by seventy broad. A hundred yards in front is a wire fence. It divides Farmer Relph's rough pasture, or intake as it is called in Cumberland, from the wood. That intake rises steeply to the left to a fairly high knoll with rocky outcrops at the top. One rock is carved into a sort of seat, and is known locally as the Roman seat. Whether the Romans ever saw it or not I don't know. From that seat lovely views of Derwent Valley may be had. Lots of people use it in the summer. The knoll is a continuation of the little plateau on which this end of the wood stands.

Fifty yards behind the hut, and somewhat higher than it, is a belt of thick spruce. It shelters the hut from the south, the stormy quarter. It was planted much later than the rest of the wood. In fact, I remember when it was planted. But it had a good start. The trees were about a yard high when they were transplanted. They suffered no setback, despite that, as they were put in with a good ball of soil at their roots.

On the right as I stand at the hut door looking out is the roadside strip. It is composed of Scots fir and larch with a few tall oaks and beeches between. When I came here, it was difficult to see through the strip, but now it is possible to see the roadway below fairly easily, although not from the door. One must walk a little way into the strip for that, owing to the contour of the ground. The road is about fifty yards distant. From it one can only with difficulty see the upper half of the hut. The road goes from the village of Braithwaite to Buttermere, one of England's beauty spots. It passes up the Vale of Newlands, which is only second to Buttermere for loveliness, and this wood follows it on the upper side for a quarter of a mile beyond those spruces behind the hut.

The roadside strip tapers down to the gate, which is almost as far away as the wire fence, but it does not stop there. Another strip carries on at the lower side of Farmer Relph's intake ; so the gateway is shaded by trees at both sides. Visitors often come to that corner where the wire fence joins the trees. They stare up at the hut, and I daresay it seems a strange sort of house to them. Now and then, one comes for a closer look.

My nearest neighbours are the people of Little Braithwaite, the hamlet below the wood, and the Relphs of Braithwaite Lodge, which is a farm round there at the end of the fell. The Lodge as, it is called locally, looks down on the village of Braithwaite, four hundred yards away. So I am not really remote from civilization, but my neighbours seldom come into the wood to see me. Occasionally, Charlie Relph ventures in to look for a lost sheep, or a villager comes to gather a few larch twigs for firewood along where some trees were felled during the war, but that is all the traffic past the hut. In summer, of course, there are visitors. They are apt to roam anywhere.

Immediately behind the hut is a little hump. It has always been there. It seems to me that some prospector, ages ago, has dug out that soil in a search for lead. Anyway, the hump is artificial, and when I came here it was growing a thicket of gorse. Gradually the gorse died ; so I planted rhododendron in its place. Those bushes have flourished, but they do not yet give shelter to the hut as the gorse did. They do, however, grow some marvellous blooms.

A little farther behind the hut are some young spruces, which I planted myself. They are sheltered from the stormy quarter by the taller belt of spruces, but they have had a sore struggle to survive. Since I planted them three years ago they have grown very little. Some of them died, because I lifted them without any great quantity of soil at their roots. Often I was not sure whether one was dead or not for weeks. Then I would go out some morning, and see the little buds forming, and know that a tree was saved. Or perhaps I would see a sickly paleness in the needles, and know that I had lost one.

I like trees very much, and if I had not been a game-keeper, I could easily have been a forester. My grand-father was a head forester ; so there is probably some rosin in my blood. But the tree that I like best beside the hut is an ancient wild cherry. It is twenty yards away. In springtime it is a mass of lovely blossom. I have often stopped to admire it when the sunlight made its fairness fairer. Some day not far distant it will be smashed by the storm. To provide a successor, I have planted another wild cherry nearby. If it gives someone as much pleasure as I have got from its venerable neighbour, I have not planted in vain. Broadly speaking, those are my immediate surroundings.

As for the more distant surroundings, there are all the Derwent Fells behind Barrow ; Swinside Fell across the dale ; Lake Derwentwater and Keswick beyond it ; the huge mass of Skiddaw to the north-east ; and behind me, the glorious fells of Newlands and Borrowdale.

The Estate

Comparatively speaking, this estate is not large, but the rented shootings which go with it, and have gone with it, make it enormous. If game could have bred on it naturally in average quantities, it might have employed a small army of gamekeepers. When I came to the hut, there were four at this end, and three at Wythop along by Lake Bassenthwaite. That number increased for a while, but now I am the sole representative. Even when keepers were fairly thick on the ground, it was impossible, and unnecessary, to patrol all the shootings. Some of that fell land is so poor that it will barely support a herdwick sheep, and that hardy animal needs no luxuries.

We had all Derwent Fells this side of the watershed ; all Bassenthwaite Lake ; half of Derwentwater ; an assortment of fields and swamps down Derwent Bog and up Newlands Valley ; a precipitous fellside clothed with oak at the Borrowdale side of Derwentwater, and Wythop, which I have already mentioned. Like the road to Tipperary, it was a long way to go. Only a small percentage of that mass is agricultural land. There are sheep on the fells ; there are cattle on the Bog, but it is a wild country, nevertheless.

Wythop is mainly Government Forest now, and is so vast as to be unsuitable for intensive game production. A legion of pheasants could be lost in those conifer woods ; and in any case, the most skilful keeper could not show birds well there, even if he could get an army of beaters to put them where he wanted. But years ago before the conifers grew so tall, pheasants were reared at Wythop, and I have attended shoots on the fellside above Bassenthwaite Lake. The keeper then was one Charlie MacDuff, a Highlander from the Blair Atholl district.

One could find a grouse or two on Wythop also, but they had to be sought on windy summits. On one pleasant August day that I remember four of us got a few brace round Lord's Seat and Wythop Hag. But the grouse shooting at any time there was far inferior to what one could get on even the poorest moors of the North Riding. There is too much room for vermin on those Lakeland fells. There are too many foxes and carrion crows. These pests hunt the low ground as well as the fells, and they are aided in their work of destruction by hunting dogs.

Therefore, if a country is not naturally adapted for game, an artificial system is introduced, that is, if the proprietor, or lessee, is a keen shooting man. And the countryside is laid out accordingly. Coverts are planted after a certain system ; low-lying, warm woods to hold the pheasants, and higher ones for rises on a shooting day. This estate was planned very successfully with that end in view.

Nowadays the hand-rearing of pheasants is forbidden by law, but apart from that, the war has made people think of other things. One can hardly imagine now that those coverts once resounded every winter evening with the chuckling of roosting pheasants ; that the pens were full of birds in the spring for egg-production ; that several keepers paraded fellside and covert, herding their charges with dogs, or hunting the vermin that preyed on them with trap and gun.

I sometimes think of those keepers, and wonder where they are now. I know where Jock Stark is. It was he who got me here, and I remember him as a kindly fellow. He is lying in Thornthwaite Churchyard. The rest are gone.

The memory of my first morning in the Lake District is still vivid with me. Jock and I left the Kennels about nine o'clock. We walked up towards Swinside Inn and Cottages in the spring sunlight. The birds were singing delightfully by the wayside, and the larch trees on Swinside Fell showed a tinge of green. Then I saw Newlands Valley for the first time. That vista of sunny fells with the blue haze of springtime on them was the most lovely sight on earth, I thought. After all those years I still think the same. Jock showed me my beat that day, and he also showed me the hut in the wood. Little did I think then that it would be my home for so many years.

Derwent Bog

Derwent Bog deserves a section to itself, because it is more interesting from a gamekeeper's point of view than the fells, beautiful though they may be. From the hut window I can see only part of it, and that part looks more like a piece of rough scrub-land than a bog. Nevertheless there is a lot of marshy ground on this visible side among those self-planted woods of birch trees. But the side nearer Skiddaw, which I cannot see for the roadside strip of this wood, is perhaps more truly bogland. It is a mass of reeds, whins and bog myrtle, and a labyrinth of ditches of varying widths and depths. The ditches, by the way, are called 'soughs' by the local population.

Newlands Beck runs down the near side of the Bog, and into it flows the Pow Beck. The Derwent flows down the far side, and connects Derwentwater with Lake Bassenthwaite. It is almost certain that, ages ago before the Bog was formed by accumulations of silt, those two lakes were one.

The whole of that tract of level territory is cut into a patchwork of big and little fields. Some are boggier than others, but none of it could be classed as good agricultural land. Quite a lot of cattle are grazed on it, however, and a certain amount of poor bog-hay is garnered each summer, if the weather permits. If the summer happens to be wet, then no hay is garnered, and apparently its want is not felt very severely. A considerable quantity of young game has perished time and again during hay and reed cutting operations in a dry summer down there by machinery and dogs. Some people take their dogs with them on those jobs, and let them harry the land around. Worse than that even is the habit that irresponsible persons have of setting the Bog alight in a dry spring. Many a hundred duck and pheasant nests have been destroyed by that careless habit. Boys are great offenders.

There are many tenants on the Bog and many proprietors. My employer owns a goodly piece of land there and has the shooting right on more, but the Bog is now mainly a pot-hunters' and a poachers' paradise. When we had jurisdiction on most of it a few years ago, there was encouragement for a gamekeeper to produce game on it, but not now. Slowly but surely, as land came into the market, through death and various other causes, somebody eager for shooting would buy it up for a song, and any land which we relinquished as too unproductive of game would be occupied immediately by gunners, who were not disappointed if they got little, so long as they could carry a gun, where formerly they had no right to shoot. Some of the pot-hunters would throw down feed to entice game on to their land, and that is a thorn in the ribs of any gamekeeper.

Nevertheless, the Bog is an interesting place. On it are pheasants, partridges, woodcock, hares, snipe, and many kinds of wildfowl. A fox occasionally takes up his abode among the reeds, where he levies heavy toll among the game population ; and otters are fairly frequent in the waterways. One may see their pad marks often in the mud, and when the snow comes, their runs from stream to stream are plainly visible.

There also used to be a fair stoat population on the Bog. They could be trapped, and were trapped, in tunnels by the beck sides, or against the stone bridges that connect many of the meadows. But stoats have not been so numerous for a year or two. When I came here, and took over the Bog as part of my beat, I could get a couple of stoats any time that I looked my tunnel traps. Not so today. Weasels have also practically disappeared. I think that the increased fox population may have something to do with their scarcity ; for I have never seen either a stoat or a weasel dead from disease.

In the clumps of holly, which are dotted here and there on the Bog, carrion crows build their nests. These birds are a terrible scourge. Over the reeds they hunt incessantly in spring and summer for the eggs and chicks of game birds. Hawks are not so inclined to nest there, but they, too, harry the Bog from the Forestry Commission woods at each side of the valley.

On the first of August, the pre-war date for the opening of wildfowl shooting, we used to go down the Bog as soon in the day as was possible ; for there was rivalry among the various shooters for the biggest bag of duck before they had all been alarmed into the lake by the shooting. Once I went down about four a.m., thinking that no one could possibly beat me, because it was still darkish. But a red-headed youth from Thornthwaite was before me. He was sitting on a bridge over Newlands Beck, waiting for enough daylight to let him see his quarry. But it was not usual for me to go after the first duck. If some guest wished to have a shot at them, we had to be content with getting on the Bog between nine and ten o'clock. There were flappers on the soughs even then, unless some farmer had disturbed them, but they provided little sport. Snipe made better shooting. They were often numerous at that time of the year, if the weather had been moist ; but now and then, for no apparent reason, there would be hardly a snipe visible. One day they would be rising at every step almost ; the next day it was difficult to find one. They had evidently found a better feeding ground somewhere.

During the warm days of August, and occasionally when the weather was not so warm, we would walk straight into the lake after the duck. My henchman, a local fellow, and I have had many exciting days among those tall reeds. We did not care how we got our duck. We fired at sitting flappers as eagerly as we fired at rapidly moving teal. We wanted duck for the Big House, and all methods were fair. Often we would shoot at a sitter, and a veritable cloud of mallard and teal would rise far out in the reeds. We would duck our heads then, and wait for the fowl to make an unwary sweep in our direction. Many a duck lost its life in that manner. But the stench of that lakehead mud, as we stirred it up on a hot day, was not pleasant; and the mosquitoes were a plague. We were perhaps crouching beneath the level of the reeds, waiting for some duck to wheel in our direction. The sun beat on our sweating skins. Mosquitoes landed on our necks. We dared not move in case the birds saw us. The itching became unbearable, and cautiously we would slap our tortured skins. On the palms of our hands were little splashes of blood, our blood. But still the brutes came, and only when we could move freely again did we get relief. For those lakehead shoots we put on our oldest clothes and boots. That mud, composed of rotting vegetation, would ruin any clothes, and the rank smell was difficult to dissipate. If the lake happened to be higher than usual, the rotting vegetation and the thick weeds floated clear of the bottom. I have walked on that vegetable raft, and felt that I was on a feather bed. That was exactly the sensation. What would have happened if one's feet had gone through the billowing mass I do not know, because the unstable thing never broke. It was tough, and I suppose that it must have also been thick.

A retriever of some sort was very valuable on the Bog. Not only did game or snipe go bang into the rushes out of sight often, if it were shot dead, and fell hard, but sooner or later something fell at the far side of a deep, wide sough, which had no bridge near at hand. A dog could save one endless trouble. One day my henchman and I lost seven head of mallard, teal and snipe, through not having a dog with us. When we lost the seventh item, we thought that home was indicated. No worth-while shooter cares to lose the game he has dropped, especially if it is dead. In that jungle of reeds one could easily stand on a dead bird and not know of it.

As the year advanced, and the wildfowl grew wary, too wary to sit on a sough or the shallow water at the lake head until a gunner approached them, we used to wait for the evening flight at the lake head. The duck passed over at dusk on their way to the feeding grounds, which might be a field of corn, or a muddy pool farther up the Bog. That flighting hour was often a test of endurance. Usually we had a look around for snipe before we took our stands, and if our feet and legs were wet, we were numb with cold before the flight was over. The best nights were the nasty ones, when the fell-tops were hidden, and ragged clouds drifted across a grey pall. If rain were falling, so much the better for the shooting, but not for the shooters. On clear nights the duck flew high, and rather strangely, they were more difficult to see than on dull nights. They made a clearer silhouette against a background of grey cloud.

Never have I shot a big bag at flighting time. The ducks come on a widish front; so the chances for one gun are lessened. I looked on half a dozen mallard as a good bag for one evening. Once I got an unexpected item, a grey goose. I was standing beside the boundary sough, staring into the heavens, when I heard the honk of geese behind me. They came on, but passed to my left, heading down-lake, and a good shot away. I fired both barrels, hoping for the best. One dropped, somewhat to my surprise. He was practically at the edge of the water when he landed, and tried to get in where he would have been safe, but I beat him to it. Then the rest of the geese came back to see what had become of their comrade. My gun was empty. What a predicament! My hands were cold and wet. I had a raincoat on, but the cartridges were in my jacket pocket underneath. I had kept them there to be dry. So I fumbled and fumbled, but I could not get to them in time. The geese wheeled just within shot of me, then with a swishing of wings and a furious honking they vanished into the gloom above the lake.

Talking of geese reminds me of a remarkable bag which I made one afternoon in the winter of 1939-40. When Paddy Gilpin, my henchman, and I set off that day, we had no thought of geese. We went down the Pow Beck simply to find a duck of some sort for the Big House larder. There were twenty-five degrees of frost that afternoon, and consequently, bitterly cold, as we reached the Bog below the Howe Farm. Snow was lying thickly everywhere. Some teal got up off the Pow Beck for a start, but my right barrel misfired, which put me off with the left ; so nothing dropped. I put the cartridge which had missed in a pocket separate from the others, and we carried on towards the Bog Hollies, a clump of trees half a mile farther down the beck. Nothing else rose, but we heard a big flock of geese honking over a field nearer the river. They settled and started to feed, or at least they appeared to feed ; for as I have said, there was thick snow everywhere.

I determined to have a try for one ; so, leaving Paddy with the gamebag, I crawled on my stomach to the nearest ditch, which was, like all the other ditches, hard frozen over. Along the ditch I slithered on my hip and elbow, pulling the gun with my right hand until I reached a cross hedge. Then I got through the wire fence that ran along beside the ditch, and crawled behind the hedge for twenty yards. The nearest goose was a long shot off, and I could get no nearer to him. Just as I was debating with myself on the best course to follow, an aeroplane came down-dale and decided everything for me. The geese rose, honking loudly with fright, and made towards Bassenthwaite Lake. I was disappointed. I got to my feet, was making back to Paddy, when I heard the geese in the distance. They appeared to be returning ; so I got down again. On they came towards me, but settled at the bottom of the meadow. That meant a fairly long crawl along the ditch and I saw that I would have to expose myself to some extent before I got into it again. However, with a lot of trouble I did get into the ditch without drawing the attention of the geese, and I slithered along the ice towards them, pushing my way all the time through snow-laden reeds. My hands were numb. Opposite the geese on the edge of the ditch was a bit of straggling thorn hedge. I was glad to see that I could have a look without being seen ; so when I arrived there I raised myself cautiously. A goose was shovelling about among the snow only twenty-five yards away, which was a good killing range. I quietly blew any possible snow out of the gun barrels, pushed two cartridges into the breech, poked the muzzles through the bottom of the hedge carefully, took a squint along the rib at the goose's head and pressed the right trigger. Horror of horrors ! there was nothing but a hollow click. The cartridge misfired, the second one that afternoon. Why the goose did not show any alarm, or even curiosity, I do not know. He went on feeding, although he must have heard the click. I have seen other, less wary creatures go away at the same warning.

I was dithering with excitement. Every second was precious, the goose might go away any time, and it was a pity to lose such a rare shot, when one was so near. So I rammed in another cartridge, aligned the gun again, and fired. The goose went flop on the snow, kicking his last, and beating his wings violently. The rest honked with surprise, some jumped backwards, but none took to wing. They all stood with upraised heads watching their unfortunate mate. They evidently had not seen me, and were therefore puzzled. Quickly I fired again and three more geese fell on the snow. This was too much for the remainder. With a fearful screaming and honking, they took to wing, but they did not go straight away even then. I had time to push one cartridge into the right breech, and as they made a circle round their fallen comrades, I brought down another. Fully alarmed, the surviving geese went off in the direction of the lake, making a terrific racket as they retreated. Then I went into the meadow and gathered my birds. Five with three shots. It will be a long time before I equal that feat again.

I looked round for Paddy, but he was nowhere visible. He had gone home, taking the gamebag with him. For a hundred yards or so I tried to carry the geese by the neck, but had to desist. They were too heavy to be carried in that manner ; so I cut an ash sapling from a nearby hedge, and hung the geese on it as a Breton carries his onions. Thus I got them home in the frosty dusk. It was a relief to get rid of them after walking the best part of two miles. That flock of geese wintered on the Bog for several years after my exploit, but they have not appeared in the last two seasons. One cannot easily explain that. Migrating geese pass over regularly, but they do not settle. When I came to the hut, there were no geese on the Bog in winter either. Then they came regularly for perhaps half a dozen times. Now they are gone once more. They were not harried here more than anywhere else ; so the reason for their non-appearance is a mystery.

When the lakes are frozen, one can often get plenty of shooting at mallard on the soughs. And when the soughs are also frozen, and even the Derwent, the Pow Beck remains open. That is a peculiar phenomenon. Never have I seen the Pow Beck frozen over. There was a hard freeze-over this year, but it came too late for duck shooting. Derwentwater and Bassenthwaite were both completely covered with thick ice in February and March. If the severe weather had come a month sooner, I could have shot a good quantity of mallard and teal. Nevertheless, I heard that a few pseudo-sportsmen had seized the opportunity to bag a lot of duck over by the Derwent. Anything that flies is unsafe while this rationing holds.

The curtailment of the wildfowl shooting season was a good measure ; for wildfowl have decreased greatly during those war years. I don't know why, unless the increase of vermin has something to do with the matter. Certainly, foxes and carrion crows, two very deadly enemies of duck, have increased.

I was looking at the Wild Birds' Protection Act in the *Kincardineshire Observer* recently, and apparently the carrion crow is protected in that county. That seems a foolish measure to me. One might as well let human beings benefit from birds' eggs as a host of black ghouls. Carrion crows may help to clean up the remains of dead sheep and other offensive stuff, but seeing that it is illegal to leave dead sheep lying about unburied, there is no object in keeping scavengers, and more especially when these scavengers will attack live sheep, even although carrion is available.

Down there by the side of Newlands Beck a little secluded wood used to stand. It was composed mainly of conifers, but in it were also some hardwoods and a lot of rhododendron bushes. On a hot summer day it was a cool, shady place ; on a cold winter day there was shelter from the biting wind. Then the beck bank burst above it during a flood. The burst was neglected for years, and the water, as it rushed through the Bog Wood, gradually killed the trees, until hardly any trace of the wood is left, except some firs on a bit of higher ground on the beck bank below where the burst was. Nowadays, the site of the burst is covered with gorse, a great bed of it, that compensates somewhat with a blaze of cadmium yellow in the springtime for the vanished wood. But I loved that charming wood, and I think of it sometimes as I go to and fro on the beck bank.

Farther down the beckside stands the Bog House. It is an old-fashioned structure, grey with age. The ridge-beam has sagged with the passage of time, and the upstairs floors have sagged also. I have been inside, when tenants were changing ; so I know. Some day the sag will bring the roof in, but recently a family lived there, apparently contented with their abode. At one time it must have been a little farm. A combined byre and barn form a continuous building with the Bog House. Some long-forgotten Cumbrian evidently eked out a meagre living on that sour, rushy land. Within living memory, it was tenanted by gamekeepers, and it would still make an ideal keeper's house, if the building were renewed somewhat.

Our land agent came to the hut yesterday with the key of the Bog House. The evacuees have apparently left it. He asked me to go down as soon as possible to see if the windows were secure; so I made my way there this morning. It was lovely as I walked down the beckside. Sunlight lay on the peaceful fells, and I felt a hint of the joy I knew on the morning when I saw the Lakeland for the first time.

The house was secure. I had a good look around the old place. Several articles of furniture had been left. A dresser was in the kitchen. A dressing table was in another room on the ground floor, and a bedstead with its mattress was upstairs in the far room, the one without a fireplace. But what a place of beams! They were old, roughly-hewn things, but they suited the house. It seemed to me that the Bog House had stood for several hundreds of years. In one little bedroom at the top of the stairs, and under the pent roof, were signs of the children who had lived there recently, little pictures, cut from magazines on the rough walls. I looked at them, and imagined how happy the children must have been in that nook, how they had snuggled down in bed as they heard the rain lash on the roof on winter nights, and how they had lain awake on summer mornings and watched the sunlight creep in through the skylight window.

I knew those evacuee children well. Often I stopped to talk with them when I was going to, or returning from, the Bog. They were nice kiddies.

II. FOLK

O NE of the most abiding friends that I have had in all my Lakeland years is Charlie MacDuff. He lives in a white-washed cottage high on the fellside above Bassenthwaite Lake, higher even than the Government Forests that clothe the steeper ground of Wythop Estate. To reach his house on foot, one must climb a diagonal road through the forest of shady spruce. It is a long pull to the top of that fell. Many a time have I proved that. To reach Charlie's house by car is a longish undertaking from here. One must turn left at the Pheasant Inn at the bottom end of Bassenthwaite Lake, then turn left again at Wythop Mill. From there one enters the upland valley of Wythop, a bleak place, but beautiful in its solitude. At the extreme end of the valley, and overlooking Derwent Vale, is the house where I have spent so many happy evenings.

Charlie was once the keeper on Wythop Estate, a rough place for a keeper, if ever there was one, but now he lives retired. To occupy his leisure he cultivates an acre or two of potatoes and hay, keeps a fair amount of poultry, a pig or two, and a milch cow. In fact he does well on his twelve acres of high-lying land. In appearance he is not startling in any way, but he is tough. I estimate his age at about seventy-odd, but he looks younger, and in all the years that I have known him, he has altered very little. Perhaps he is a little harder of hearing. That is all. His hair, what there is of it, is fine and sandy. His eyes are blue, and he is about middle height. Rheumatism is the only ailment that has troubled him for many years, and that only in one shoulder.

It does, however, prevent him from using a gun easily. The rheumatism is undoubtedly a legacy from a shooting accident, which he had as a young man in his native Perthshire. Charlie has told me several times of that near-tragedy.

He and a farm servant were apparently ferreting rabbits in a sand hole one Saturday afternoon. The ploughman was a novice with the gun, but he begged Charlie for a shot. Charlie handed the greenhorn the loaded gun, took the ferret to the burrow, and without warning, received a charge of shot in his back. The cartridge-wad and all sorts of muck were in the wound, but there was no permanent injury, unless the rheumatism can be called a permanent injury. It afflicts the shoulder nearest the old wound. Charlie said that when he was coming to himself he heard the doctor say : 'By Jove ! the laddie's a tough ane.' I am convinced that the laddie was a tough ane.

Before I had seen Charlie's abode, I had often seen Charlie himself at our shootings near Derwentwater. He came with a dog to pick up pheasants, but I had never much talk with him. However, Jock Lowe and I set off one lovely Sunday afternoon to visit Louthwaiteside, the MacDuff homestead. Bassenthwaite Lake was serenely beautiful as we went along the road on the left-hand shore, and Skiddaw at the far side was hazy in the sunlight. We had only a vague idea where Charlie lived. None of us knew to leave the main road at Beck Wythop, and climb up the steep, fell path. So we carried on until we were practically at the Pheasant Inn, three miles or so farther on than we need have gone. Then we took to the fell. We got to the top, but saw no sign of Louthwaiteside. Then we circled the fell top, and after miles of unnecessary wandering in the hot sun, we saw Charlie MacDuff's house below us. It was a cheering sight.

When we got into the yard, I stopped back a few yards from the door. I was inclined to be shy. Jock was not bothered with that drawback, luckily. He presented himself at the door and was immediately asked in. A moment later

he came out and took me in also. Mrs. MacDuff was out
visiting some of her friends, but Charlie set us down to a
good tea. We enjoyed that feed after those hot hours on the
fell. After the meal we sat in for a talk. Piping cropped up
in the conversation somehow, and Charlie produced a set
of full-ivory mounted pipes which had belonged to his
father, once a piper to the Duke of Atholl. Charlie himself
was no piper, but I soon had the drones humming in
Louthwaiteside kitchen. They were good pipes.

Since that day long ago I have been in the kitchen at
Louthwaiteside often. I have made the old building ring
with the sound of the pipes. In the parlour, the photo of
Peter MacDuff, dressed in Highland garb, hangs on the
wall, but he will play those pipes no more. He was over
ninety when he died. Charlie has the look of longevity
about him, too.

I have gone up to Louthwaiteside on all sorts of evenings.
There were balmy, summer evenings when I found Charlie,
his sons, Gordon and Charlie, and daughter, Helen, busy
among the fragrant hay in a field before the house. Charlie,
by the way, always has had that croft, even when he was a
keeper. On other evenings I found them all sitting before a
cheery fire, defying the blackness of the winter night. I was
always made welcome to the circle. What talks we have had
beside the fire ! We never thought of breaking the ceilidh
until midnight had struck, and often we talked into the
small hours. After supper I played a tune or two on the
pipes. Mrs. MacDuff is particularly fond of pipe music.
These were delightful evenings. I never grudged the five
mile walk back to the hut. The dark-looming fells were
friendly after I had partaken of Louthwaiteside hospitality.

Occasionally the dawn of a summer day has been breaking
as I neared Braithwaite. I have seen the early thrushes sitting
on a dewy hedge along near Thornthwaite, pouring out
their lovely melody. Across the dale was the pale dawn
above Skiddaw. A cock would crow in the yard at Lanefoot,
and I would see a poaching cat slinking homewards to

prove that it had not been hunting the fields for nestlings and young rabbits. Up the lonning towards the hut I would see the dawn grow brighter to my left above Keswick, and as I climbed from the gate in the last lap, the rabbits would scurry into the wood. Then I would enter the silent hut, and sleep for an hour or two. When I woke again, it was full Sabbath daylight.

Trespassers

Broadly speaking, trespassers may be divided into three classes. There are those who would not willingly do any sort of harm; there are those who are indifferent as to whether they do harm or not, and there are those who trespass solely for some personal gain. Among the latter are the flower and fruit gatherers, the bird nesters, the wood lifters, and the poachers. But all of them, even the most courteous, are liable to do some harm as soon as they enter forbidden territory. They are also liable to sustain harm themselves, though it may be inflicted unwittingly. No doubt, many a gamekeeper has paled with fear when he has fired a shot in the recesses of a wood where no one is normally seen, and suddenly found a trespasser standing almost in the line of his fire. Most gamekeepers are careful not to gamble with powder and shot, but when one is taking a tricky shot at, say, a woodcock, a momentary lapse may easily occur.

An incident happened to me the other evening with a trespasser, which could hardly even be called a lapse, because the chances of a trespasser's being where I later found him were so remote as hardly to merit consideration. Snow was lying knee-deep around the hut. It had been lying for weeks, and I had been making use of the hard weather to remove some of the numerous carrion crows that infest the Lake District. I had a dead sheep lying fifty yards from the bedroom window of the hut, and whenever a carrion landed on it or near it I shot it; or to be more correct, I shot at it, because fifty yards is rather an extreme range for my weapon and ammunition.

About six o'clock on this particular evening I saw a carrion settle near the sheep. Carefully I lowered the window an inch at a time. There was an explosion, but to my chagrin, the crow flew away. I took a step towards the window quickly, and fired the second barrel at it flying, which made it waver. Then I rushed out to mark it down, but was a little late. The carrion had disappeared. When I got to the top of the rise behind the hut, and beyond the belt of spruces, I heard a cracking of sticks up the wood. There was a village man looking for firewood. To say the least, I was alarmed. I went back to the hut without finding the crow, and had a look at my angle of fire. The shot had been about the right (or wrong) elevation, but somewhat to the trespasser's low side. If it had hit him, he might not have been badly damaged. That was not the point, however. I did not know he was there, nor did I even dream that anyone could be there on such a bitter evening.

Another time many years ago I was shooting rabbits in a large mass of bracken. My spaniel was chasing them across the bare patches, and I was snapshooting as they disappeared. After I had knocked over about four, a head appeared above the fronds a dozen yards away. I got a fright. The youth had been comfortably reading a book under the cover while the shots racketed around him. I told him that he would live longer, if he showed himself in future, when shots were being fired near him. But he was much less alarmed than I was. He even begged a shot at a fencing post on the wood edge.

Once a bevy of three girls appeared suddenly at the end of the ride at the top of this wood, when I was hunting pigeons, or vermin, I forget which. I shuddered as I thought how a bird might have swooped out of a spruce, and gone along the ride in their direction. Two of the girls were dark-skinned Asiatics of some sort. The other was their opposite. She was fair with blue eyes, and I learned later that she was a Norwegian. I got no encouragement, when I told them that they were trespassing. In their own countries, I suppose, there was no such thing as trespassing. At least, I got that impression.

Trespassers often pass the hut. They seem to think that this path in the wood leads on to the open fell, instead of which, it returns to the Newlands Valley-Buttermere road along at the far gate. They are generally intrigued to find that a man can live in a hut permanently. Many a pleasant talk I have had with some of these trespassers. When I tell them how long I have lived here, they are astonished. They cannot understand how anyone can live without the amenities of our near-civilization. Then they try to supply a reason for such eccentricity.

The most incongruous trespasser that I have seen came past the hut one summer morning at six o'clock as I was mixing a big basin of pheasant feed. He was dressed in a silk hat and a well-cut morning coat. In London at ten o'clock in the morning he might have passed unnoticed, but he was a kenspeckle figure, indeed, in a Lakeland wood at that early hour. He wished to get to Barrow lead mine ; so I directed him, and that was the last I ever saw of him, but I concluded later that he was connected with a company that was trying to re-open some of those old workings.

Trespassers need not break fences, or lift anything, or leave gates open to do harm. Often I have had my plans upset by people who were wandering where they had no right to be. For instance, I have perhaps got an order for rabbits suddenly, which have to be delivered the following morning. I take my gun to a place where rabbits usually feed in the evenings, and where I can approach them easily. Not a rabbit to be seen. I look around and find someone enjoying the beauties of nature from an unusual viewpoint, or perhaps merely wandering about for no apparent reason. The trespasser in such a case is not aware of his nuisance value, and may consider me unreasonable when I ask him to depart, but he has, nevertheless, upset my calculations.

I. The Author's home in cherry blossom time

II. The Author at the door of a rearing-field hut

III. Lovely Newlands Valley

IV. Derwent Bog

Where pheasants are roosting, a trespasser may do harm by walking along a woodland ride in the gloaming with his hands in his pockets. The pheasants fly away, but do not go to roost again. They jug on the ground, and are killed by a prowling fox. Thus the trespasser has encompassed their deaths just as much as if he had shot them.

Occasionally, I meet a trespasser who gets heated about the People's Rights. What he really means is that he has a right to go where he wishes. He is not usually a person who is interested at all in the rights of other people. But fortunately those ones are not numerous.

Beaters

When these woods were well stocked with hand-reared pheasants, we used to employ about thirty beaters on big shooting days to drive the birds forward to the guns, and to act as stops at points where the pheasants were inclined to run out quietly from the beat.

About a third of the beaters, the best of them, came from the dale farms. Another third of fair quality came from the village. The remainder, a mixed lot, came from Keswick. They were recruited at the Labour Exchange. We tried to divide those beaters out, so that there were good ones among the duds, but even then a shooting day was always something of a purgatory. It is not easy to control beaters in dense cover, and it is impossible to watch individuals. Some over-excited beater would press forward to see what was happening when a volley of shooting went off at the covert end. He would go quite heedless of the rest, until a cloud of back-flying pheasants announced to us that something was wrong. If the guns saw those birds there were frowns and mutterings. But the keeper got blamed for those mishaps. He ought to have exercised more control over his beaters.

Mistakes can occur on comparatively open ground just as easily as in thick cover if the beaters are thick-headed, or indifferent. When this wood was shot, I used to take about a dozen men soon after daybreak round to the back of the fell to drive in any birds that might have gone there after leaving their roosting places here. I lined them up half a mile back to make certain that I missed nothing, and gave each beater strict instructions to stop when he reached the path above the wood. I also warned them not to make a noise at the wood edge in case they alarmed the birds before the guns arrived to take up their stands at the up-valley end. There were perhaps a thousand pheasants in the wood, and pheasants are like sheep in one respect. They are apt to follow the leader blindly. If one bird had been alarmed out of the wood, a score, or a hundred might have followed it. So I impressed on the beaters every shooting morning the importance of silence, and the necessity of stopping on the path until I arrived.

One morning we went through our routine, preliminary drive-in. A few birds flew into the wood from the bracken on the shoulder of the fell, and I went along to collect the beaters, leaving one to act as a stop about every fifty yards. Half-way along I missed a beater. I asked the nearest ones if they knew where he had gone. They replied that he had carried on over the wall into the wood. Later I found him below the wood on the Newlands Valley road. Some loaders had intercepted him, otherwise he might have gone on until the beck stopped him. Luckily, he had not put any birds out of the covert, but that was not his fault. One stands appalled at such stupidity. Obviously the fellow had not listened to what I told him, nor did he bother to interpret his function in the scheme of things. He was started by someone, and he was stopped by someone ; and between those two acts he plodded on vacantly.

On another shooting day an irresponsible youth started the drive before the guns were in their positions. He had a lot more in his skull, however, than the vacant plodder. In fact, he was a little too cute. It was not for a year that I discovered who had sent that false signal whistle.

We were lined up on that particular morning, waiting for the guns to get into their places at the far end of the wood, which is near Derwentwater. Clearly came the signal to start the drive, a peculiar whistle of three notes. I was suspicious. The signal was perfectly imitated, but the time was not quite right. I did not expect the guns to be in position for at least another quarter of an hour. However, when the signal came again, I started. Great consternation when we got half-way through the wood ! We were stopped. Why had we started ? In vain I protested that the signal had gone. Bunkum ! I ought to have made certain that the guns were in their positions, and so on. I am not very clear today how I could have made certain without making a detour of half a mile round the covert, and if I had gone to that trouble, I probably would have found that the signal was genuine. Then what ? Another row for ignoring the signal. If I had found the practical joker that morning, he would have had an alarming five minutes.

The beaters were expected to bring their own lunch, but the Big House always sent out an urn of excellent coffee, and a gallon or two of beer came from the inn, with which to wash it down. The beer I never tasted, but the real connoisseurs assured me that it was poor stuff. Nevertheless, the cask was always emptied. There were several old stagers who saw to that. They made for the cask as soon as they were able, and swilled away until they were called off. One tall, splay-footed veteran used to pour the beer down his gullet as one pours water down a sink. There was no apparent act of swallowing the liquor in gulps. Up went the tankard full ; down it came empty. I was fascinated. Years of assiduous practice must have gone to achieve such mastery. If he had gulped like an ordinary person, he would have lost precious seconds in his boozing marathon. With all the beer he had, I never saw him even slightly tipsy, but others who had not his constitution were occasionally merry. Some were at times decidedly fuddled.

Although a few of the beaters were lacking in acumen,

they were, on the whole, honest. But a certain small pro-
portion had to be watched carefully. Pheasants, which had
flown away wounded from the guns, were often picked up
dead by the beaters in another drive. That was a temptation,
because they were not always seen with the birds by a
keeper ; and it was a simple matter to push them into a
rabbit hole, or cover them with a heap of dead leaves, until
the day's shooting was over, when they could be collected
by the wily beater. I have heard often of that trick, but only
once was I certain that it actually had been practised. One
evening after the last drive a beater told me that one of the
others had killed a wounded cock pheasant among some
bramble bushes during the drive. He had carried it openly
for a bit, then it had suddenly vanished. I went to the
beater to find out what had become of the bird, but he
denied having it. By this time the informer was on his way
home, and it was unluckily the last shoot of the season ; so
I never got to the bottom of the affair.

It will be a long time before the tapping of sticks is
heard in those woods again. That motley crowd, I am
afraid, will never meet me at the cross-roads as the pheasants
fly from their roosts at the break of day. I will see them in
future only in my dreams. But I am not sure that I feel
sorry. They were a jovial lot, but they lacked discipline.
And their irresponsibility made me often anxious.

Poachers

Poachers are not nice people, as a rule, but there are grades
of poachers just as there are grades of other law-breakers.
Some are comparatively mild, and poach only occasionally
when the chance presents itself ; others are vicious, depraved
humans who would rather poach than work honestly, and
who would resist arrest with any weapon which happened
to be handy.

Many people see something romantic in the poacher. He
is often imagined as a daring freebooter, a shrewd fellow

who is more than a match for keepers, and who knows all
there is to be known about wild things. The burglar doesn't
get anything like the same consideration. He is a menace to
ordered society, and his depredations are not at all romantic.
But actually there is little difference between the poacher and
the burglar. They express their anti-social inclinations
differently, that's all. If more people owned coverts and
rabbit shoots, the poacher would be more often classed as a
common nuisance, which, in fact, he really is.

Ever since I came to the hut I have had to cope with
poachers, both by day and night. It is only seldom, however, that I have been in Court with them, but that does
not argue inability to catch poachers. I have caught literally dozens. The reason why they have not all landed in
Court is because I have found that the occasional poacher
will stop, if he is once caught. The more hardened ones, I
am sorry to say, have eluded me, or I have got them with
insufficient evidence. It is much better to let a poacher go
than to lose a case.

Poaching has many phases. There are poachers with the
gun ; there are poachers with the ferret and net ; there are
poachers with the trap and snare ; there are poachers with
the wire-netting pheasant catcher ; there are poachers with
the long net ; there are poachers with the bird net ; there
are poachers with the lurcher, and there are poachers with
a lot of other less-known devices. The silliest method is, I
think, snaring and trapping, because the keeper can be
waiting at the right place, certain of a catch, if the poacher
returns.

I find that the favourite method of poaching rabbits is by
ferret and nets. It is quite a good way of getting a few
rabbits, but ferrets are uncertain creatures. They often stick
up, and keep the poacher in an uncomfortable place indefinitely. Several times I have picked up ferrets which
have been lost by poachers. Some of them were wild after
long liberty, but they generally became tame again with
gentle usage.

Night poachers I detest. One never knows what may happen in a scrimmage in which firearms are involved, and pheasant poachers at night are usually armed. I have often hunted poachers at night in these woods, and stopped their poaching, but I have never got to grips with a pheasant poacher during the hours of darkness. I have been near enough one many a time to hear the faint crackle of twigs as he slipped away, and now and then I have kept him guessing so much that he did not dare leave the covert until daylight. Even that helps. No poacher can feel at all comfortable, if he knows that the keeper is alert. He may bag a pheasant, but he is compelled either to clear off immediately, or lie low for hours.

It is very difficult, indeed, to locate a poacher at night if he has the nerve and a brutal indifference to cold to lie still in a thicket for hours. A good dog, I daresay, could rout him out, but I never had a dog that would grow excited at a hidden man.

Alarm guns are useful in a pheasant covert. Often they save a pheasant, as well as giving the poacher's exact position away. I used them both for foxes and poachers when we reared a lot of pheasants. For the latter I set the trip wire about a yard above the ground. A fox can pass under a wire set at that height without springing the gun. Usually I set those guns to intercept anyone going along a ride, or avenue, in the wood, but I soon found that poachers became aware that the rides were dangerous. They moved about among the trees, instead, although the travelling there is always more difficult. When I discovered that move, I extended the trip wires, so that they would be pulled unwittingly by anyone among the trees. There was one drawback. On windy nights a waving tree, or a falling branch, would set the gun off.

The cartridges for those alarm guns were blanks, and were loaded with black powder, which gives a heavy report, almost like a blasting shot. It was seldom that I failed to hear a gun go off. In the hut here the explosion was as distinct as if I had been outside. In fact, on windy nights the explosion was more distinct inside. Rather strangely, I always appeared to be awake when an alarm gun fired. The report must have wakened me almost always, but it was so distinct that I seemed to have been lying awake waiting for it. And if both my ears were clear of the pillow at the time, I could usually tell which gun had gone off. Often, however, I have gone out in the middle of a freezing winter night to find out why an alarm gun had fired, and found that every gun was standing. I knew then that the shot had been fired by a poacher.

Occasionally poachers are betrayed by something beyond their own control. They never know when a flock of pigeons will rise in a noisy mass from the tree-tops, and go whistling in all directions. Pigeons do not fly at night from choice. The scream of a blackbird in the darkness as it leaves a bush near the poacher is another indication to the alert keeper that all is not well. And pheasants rising from the ground in unusual places is a certain sign that something or somebody has disturbed them in their customary roosting place.

One moonlight night I was coming from Keswick on foot. As I was passing Ullock Moss some pigeons rose about a hundred and fifty yards inside the wood. I stood for a few minutes, listening ; and when no other noise became audible, I walked on, half-convinced that an owl had appeared among them. Then a couple of pheasants got up from the roadside farther on. That made me quite certain that poachers were about ; so I walked back quietly along the road verge, until I came to a convenient gap in the hedge, where I got into the wood. I stalked cautiously forward among the spruces, and when I got to the limit of them, I stood stock still. There were then some larches beyond the spruces, and it was fairly evident that the pheasants had been roosting in them. Any pheasants roosting in the spruces would hardly see the poachers, and the poachers would certainly not have seen them ; so I waited.

An hour went past, but still I remained immobile. It was freezing hard. I began to feel shivery, and finally I moved and went home. It was possible, I thought, that the poachers had seen me approach, and had quietly slipped away. But I was wrong in that surmise. A year later a fellow stopped me in Keswick, and told me of that night's happenings. The poachers had seen me come into the wood in the moonlight, and had hidden. If they were as cold as I was, they did not have a comfortable time. There were only a few birds in that wood then, otherwise I would have stopped the whole night. As it was, I slipped away as quietly as I could ; so I have no idea how long the poachers remained in their hiding place.

At one time there were branches of hardwood trees hanging over the road at the side of Ullock Moss. Pheasants roosted on these branches, and were, no doubt, a temptation to poachers. One night I heard a light gun go off in the direction of Ullock Moss ; so I proceeded to the wood, thinking that some poachers were in it. I did not think of the roadway as a poaching stance. It was a moonless night, and I had difficulty in walking about without making a noise, but eventually, I saw the glow of a cigarette near the signpost where the road divides to Newlands and Buttermere. There was a hedge between me and the smoker ; so I could get no nearer to him then the width of the road and the grass verge. He himself was invisible to me in the darkness. I waited a few seconds, then someone joined the smoker. Some low conversation took place, and I recognised the voices. Habitual poachers were there. They seemed to be uneasy, and one went off in the direction of the village. The other stopped by the signpost, and was joined by someone on a bike, obviously the shooter. I recognised his voice also. They had a confab for a few minutes, then they followed the one who had gone first.

A keeper has very little power on the highway ; so, instead of following them, I went to a nearby house to ring up the Police. There I got a setback ; the phone was only on a private line. I asked for a bike. No lights. That was enough. I set off on foot, but the poachers got home first. I knew them all, but that was nothing. I had seen no dead game, if they had any ; nor could I actually say I had seen the men. But they must have suspected my presence in the wood, because they came no more to shoot pheasants there.

I often thought when I was afflicted with pheasant poachers at night that a camera, set with synchronized flashlight apparatus, would get a picture of the marauder, if nothing else. There is one drawback to that idea. If the poacher suspected that no one was near the camera, he might take it away, or damage it. But apart from that possibility, the idea would work. Wary animals are photographed successfully at night ; so why not poachers ? Once I photographed a poacher in daylight. He was out with a greyhound looking for a hare to course when I found him in a meadow near the railway. He said that he was searching for mushrooms when I challenged him, but I pointed out that the field was the poorest one for mushrooms he could have chosen. The grass was too long. While I was speaking, I pulled out my camera, and took a snap of him and his hound. He apparently did not realise the significance of my action, as he stood quite still with the hound in front of him. A train passed just then. I noticed that the driver was leaning out of his cab, and looking interestedly in our direction ; so I noted the number of the locomotive mentally. Then I told the greyhound man that I had a strong case against him. That alarmed him somewhat, and he made off to his caravan, which was in a field nearby. This happened on a Saturday afternoon. Before Monday morning he had vanished, although I believe he intended to stop in his camp until the end of summer. I still have his photograph, but I bluffed him into bolting. On Monday I went over to Swaledale for the grouse season ; so I would have been unable to proceed with a case against him, even if I had wished to do so.

I have found the camera useful in other ways. For instance,

twice I have found a wire-netting pheasant catcher set on my ground. I took a photo of both. On another occasion I found a plundered pheasant nest in a hedge bottom on a certain farm. There was a stone in the middle of it. The camera recorded the fact for anyone who might not have been able to visit the place.

When we had a lot of pheasants in those woods, a great deal of petty poaching went on among people who could not ordinarily be classed as poachers. Cars sometimes drew up along the side of this wood when the drivers saw a bird poking at the wire-netting, and stones were flung. Once I saw a catapult used, but I never saw a stone reach its billet.

One car poacher had a rifle. I was at the top of the wood that afternoon, when I heard the report of a .22 down by the roadway. I ran down the ride, and before I emerged from the trees, I saw a fellow taking aim over the fence at a half-grown pheasant, twenty yards from him on a bit of open ground. He was steadying himself on a post, and the muzzle of the rifle was almost in line with me. I waited until he had fired his shot, not because I wanted him to kill the pheasant and so make a better case, but because I feared that if he were suddenly alarmed, he might fire at me. So he fired, and missed. Immediately I rushed forward. He gave a yell of terror, and ran along the road to the car, which was standing with its engine running, jumped on the footboard and an accomplice drove off with the poacher still hanging on outside. I got to the fence in time to take the number of the car, which I wrote down on my gun stock, but it was probably a false one, because nothing happened after I reported the affair.

The first poachers I ever had in Court were rabbiters. I got their ferret, which came out of the burrow after they left on my approach ; so I had a bit of good evidence. The principal was an old chap with eighty-three convictions to his discredit. My case made eighty-four. One would have thought, taking his age into consideration, that his eighty-fourth would have been his last, but Sandy Coutts, the river watcher, got him a few years later with a salmon which he had illegally gaffed. That was his final conviction. Somehow he came to the conclusion that poaching did not pay, or his health may have been failing. He died not long after that eighty-fifth conviction, anyway. That old warrior's nose was flattened by the blows he had got in many a scrimmage. In his youth he had been a tough fellow, and had resisted arrest by every possible means. But there was nothing romantic about him. The fact that he finished up with eighty-five convictions showed that he had little acumen. His satellites in my case were two lads. They benefited by experience apparently. I never found them poaching again, nor did I ever hear of their doing so.

A great deal of poaching is done brazenly in daylight with the gun. A gamekeeper cannot run to every shot, as a farmer here and there is always letting a gun off. Only when the shooting is in an unusual place does one go to the scene of operations at once. But occasionally, out of curiosity, I have gone to see who was shooting in a place where a legitimate shooter might have been expected, and found someone poaching quite openly. Very often the poaching was done from the road. Sometimes the poacher pleaded ignorance of the law. One such case occurred up the dale a few summers ago. The sportsman was a visitor. He and his mate had spent several evenings shooting rabbits from the roadway before I came on them. They had a good bagful of rabbits, and the shooter told me that he was entitled to shoot from the highway. Whether he actually believed that or not I don't know, but I convinced him that it was an offence even to discharge a firearm on the highway.

Poaching has increased a lot since rationing became strict. Rabbits bear the brunt of the attack. At last the poacher has an excuse that carries some conviction. In pre-war days he used to protest that he poached for sport, but he doesn't bother with that pretence any more.

Gipsies

It isn't often nowadays that I rise to see the blue smoke of a gipsy camp fire trailing above the hazel bushes of the Watery Lonning. At one time that was a common occurrence; too common. And it meant that I had to interview certain members of the Romany tribe before the day was out.

Despite its name, the Watery Lonning is not always watery. Only when Newlands Beck is in flood, is the name justifiable. It is a sunken lane, overhung with hardwood trees and lined with hazel bushes, and its principal function is to provide a rough road to most of the Bogland meadows that lie towards the river Derwent; although, as I have already said, it also is a getaway for water in times of flood. This top end near the main road is an ideal camping site for gipsies. There is plenty of wood at hand for fires, there are rabbits nearby in Clocker Howe, and a few hares on the Bog; and the bushes provide cover from the prying eyes of policemen and gamekeepers. I daresay that many a rabbit has been stewed in the Watery Lonning.

Most gipsies have cars now; so camping down there isn't so popular as it used to be, and anyway, the Local Authorities have tightened up their regulations lately, but at one time I had to move on caravan-dwellers or bivouackers almost every week. Sometimes the gipsies would move off at the first warning; sometimes they would defy one for days until the village policeman took a hand in the affair. Even when he told them to get going, they would often snatch an extra day or two, but they always disappeared before a summons could be served.

The better class of gipsy had a clean, bright caravan, and if the lurcher had been absent, I might have been inclined to let that type remain indefinitely, but the lurcher was never absent. The worst kind of gipsy had merely a tarpaulin bivouac under the bushes. Inside the bivouac was perhaps an old mattress, or a layer of straw. And the owner fitted the squalid picture usually. He was quite definitely of a low type; probably a methylated spirits drinker, but at any rate, never clean either in person or surroundings.

One Saturday evening I went to one of the bivouac kind, and, as was my custom, I asked him as civilly as possible when he intended to move. He turned round from the camp fire, where some tea was boiling in a black tin, and said insolently: 'I'll move when I'm . . . well ready.' That riled me somewhat; so I told him to be off by Monday morning, otherwise he and his gear would land on the road. Instantly his manner changed. He became soft-soapy. Like most gipsies of the less-intelligent kind, he thought that anyone who spoke reasonably was a softy.

But even when dealing with the best of gipsies, firmness is necessary. At least, I have found that so. Let them see any sign of nervousness, and your authority wanes; so it behoves a keeper to march into a gipsy encampment as if he were going into his own house, although dirty looks and growling dogs may greet him on every side. Contrary to general belief, gipsies are more often timid than not. They may, if they have a grouch against you, hint that their sons or their brothers or some of their other relations are boxers or wrestlers, but seldom does anything happen. Once in Clocker Howe beside the Watery Lonning a gipsy boosted up his mate, a youth of twenty, so much as a wrestler that I took him on. What a fraud! The wrestler was actually the puniest fellow I have ever had hold of. He went down like an empty bag.

There was another gipsy, however, who was rather an exception. He was coursing with a lurcher among some whins down by the beckside one evening. When I went to him, he pulled out a long knife, and threatened to do me in, but seeing that he kept moving off as he uttered his threats, I didn't bother with him. A few days later I found him gathering sticks. He was very polite then. Whether he had forgotten to bring the knife with him I don't know, but his talk almost gave me the impression that we were old pals. And that swift change to oiliness is, I think, a gipsy characteristic. I remember one particularly oily chap down in the Watery Lonning who assured me that he would be only too glad to move on when one of his caravan wheels came back from the smithy. I looked round, and sure enough one of the far wheels was off. It was obvious that the poor fellow was stuck ; so I left him with the hope that his wheel would be repaired soon. Day after day passed, and the caravan still remained. Then I met the policeman, and he asked me why it hadn't been moved on. I told him of the gipsy's misfortune, but he merely laughed. 'That's an old dodge,' he said. 'The wheel's very likely inside the caravan. But I'll see what I can do.' Next day the caravan was gone. The wheel had come back from the smithy.

No gipsy children ever went to the village school when they were in the district, and I suppose that they never went to any school, but only once did I have any proof of illiteracy among Romanies. One morning a swarthy chap of about twenty-five asked me to read an inscription on a metal box for him. The inscription was 'British Made.' Rather astonishing!

Despite everything, I have had some interesting talks with gipsies, if they were camping in legitimate places, I always like to know where they have been, and what they have seen ; for when all is said and done, the best of them lead more colourful lives than we people of fixed abode, although perhaps they aren't much of an asset to the countryside.

Farmers

In the course of my job here I have had many dealings with farmers. We have mutual interests. In fact, if my Unemployment Insurance card is any indication, I am an agricultural worker. And I regard Agriculture as the main industry in any country, despite the fact that farmers have not always been classed very high in the social scale. But that snobbish outlook has altered a lot in recent years. The man who produces food has become important. In the future he may become even more important.

On the whole, I would be inclined to regard farmers as a pessimistic race. Perhaps their lives are too close to capricious Nature for levity. Even in the best of times, stock are always dying or ailing ; foxes take toll of lambs ; insect pestilence affects the crop yield ; floods destroy or carry away what is left ; and rabbits, pigeons, carrion crows, moles, hares, rats and sometimes pheasants, add their quota of worry. No wonder the poor farmer takes a serious outlook on life.

My job in recent years has been mainly concerned with the destruction of those mammalian and feathered pests ; so I know what damage they all can do, if they become too numerous in the wrong place. I add that last clause, because rabbits in the right place can be a distinct asset to the country while this food scarcity lasts. But I shall say more about rabbits.

If a farmer is annoyed by the depredations of any of those pests that can be classed as *Ferae Naturae*, he has only to lodge a complaint with the county Agricultural Committee. They will send along a pests officer to investigate the damage ; and if the complaint is justified, the pests officer will take steps to remove the nuisance. But first of all he will ask the farmer what he has done to combat the nuisance himself. A farmer who invokes the aid of a pests officer has usually done little in the matter ; so, if the pests are actually living on the farm, the officer sends a man to destroy them, but the farmer is obliged to pay the man's wages while he employs him ; for he is actually the farmer's employee as long as he remains on the farm. On the other hand, the farmer is allowed to take the kill, and to sell it, if it be marketable. In the case of rabbits, the return may be considerable, and may even show a profit.

However, if the pests are coming into the farm from adjoining land over which the farmer has no control, such as woodlands that belong to the landlord, the pests officer will notify the landlord to have them destroyed. He will allow a reasonable time to elapse, and if the order is not complied with, he will send a man, or men, to do the job, and the expense of the destroying will be borne by the landlord.

Now, I have found that farmers do not always interpret their own position towards pests properly. With regard to rabbits, they will ask me to get rid of them, even although the rabbits are living entirely on their own ground. And their asking will not always be polite. At the same time they will often give several persons permission to shoot on their land, and that permission may only be verbal, which is all contrary to the law. Moreover, that sort of thing is a source of anxiety to me, because I never know whether the shooters are poachers or not, or whether they will nullify my efforts if they are not poachers. A genuine pests destroyer gets the jumps, when he finds all sorts of people acting as amateur pests destroyers in the area where he is operating.

I have gone to set snares in a field and found snares already set there; I have gone to ferret rabbit burrows and found that they had already been ferreted. All that acts against efficiency. After a time the forestalled, legitimate pests destroyer leaves the amateur to have a free hand. Then comes the trouble. The amateur only wants rabbits when they are worth money. He is not interested in killing milky does and month-old rabbits; so he abandons his pests destruction about the beginning of April or sooner. And that is the very time when rabbits begin to do real damage. They attack the sprouting corn crops. A little later, in the hotter days, they become a menace to turnip seedlings, especially when they are newly thinned. It is then that the legitimate, efficient man is called to the rescue. He tries to forget the shabby treatment which he got during the winter, and wrestles gamely to save the crops, although the rabbits are, commercially speaking, not worth bothering about.

V. Ferrets : mother explores while the young feed

VI. Rabbiting : waiting for a clear shot

VII. Fox : scourge of the fells

VIII. Gamekeeper's Gibbet

Then as soon as rabbits become valuable again, the amateur appears with ferret and nets, snares and gun to rid the land of pests, and incidentally, to make money. I have experienced all that, but I seldom get heated up about it. Instead I try to make the rabbit population so small that the amateur does not get a fat rake-off. At the same time, I avoid clashing with him in the winter.

Of course, if rabbits are coming from woods on to farm land, the estate pests destroyer is entirely liable. It is his bounden duty to reduce their numbers. I have worked for weeks round one menaced field when there was no return for the labour. But friction with the farmer was avoided and valuable food was saved. Only once that I can remember have I received official notice through our agent to destroy rabbits. Those rabbits were supposed to be coming off a fellside to a couple of small oat fields. I was somewhat surprised at this, because the corn everywhere was quite well-grown, and rabbits usually do most damage while the shoots are tender. In addition to that, there were very few rabbits in that locality.

One day after dinner I went over to see the fields. They had been ploughed out of old lea, and the soil was light, fellside stuff. Moreover, there was a drought at the time. First of all I saw that the oat crop in the higher field was stunted and thin. By the way, that happened often where old grassland had been ploughed out. On closer examination, I saw oat roots lying on the surface of the sandy soil, and later I found that the fence at the top of the field had been recently repaired with rails. Obviously sheep had been getting into the field. The lower field showed more signs of sheep. There were droppings on the endrigs. Only one rabbit run was visible ; it led to the top field. So I made no attempt to kill the non-existent rabbits. The farmer admitted that lambs had been getting into the fields, but denied all knowledge of the complaint. He was a decent fellow, and I believed him. Someone had probably seen the stunted crops, and had decided to be patriotic.

D

III. ANIMALS

Rabbits   Moles   Foxes

Cats   Stoats   Weasels

Hedgehogs   Dogs   Ferrets

I⊤ is my opinion that the rabbit is a much-maligned creature, at the present day, at any rate, when all food is valuable. That he can be a pest is an undoubted fact, but there are pests and pests. In a flock-raising country like the Lake District, sheep can be dreadful pests, although they are never classed officially in that category. Yet, in the last few years, when more and more land has been intensively cultivated, I have seen half a dozen sheep do more damage in a green-crop field in one night than a hundred rabbits could have accomplished in a year. And the rabbit as a pest must not be classed with the rat who destroys far more than he eats, and is a disease-carrier into the bad bargain.

The fact that it is difficult to keep rabbits within bounds, and difficult also for any one man to establish complete ownership over them, unless they are fenced in with wire-netting, are two reasons why rabbits are usually regarded as pests. Then they are cunning creatures, and troublesome to bring to the market ; but it is wrong, I think, to say that they are entirely an economic loss. On the contrary, they can be the only source of revenue on waste land, and a help to the nation's food supply.

There are many ways of killing rabbits. Some are cruel ; some are not quite so cruel, but perhaps a well-directed shot is the only really painless method. Recently a new version of the steel trap has been evolved, which is said to kill the rabbit outright, but whether it will live up to its inventor's claims is not yet clear. I will be glad if a humane trap has at last been invented, but I will also be surprised if it is as effective as the old gin, which is at the moment the only real rabbit-reducer, if used by an expert.

Rubber-jawed traps have been tried, so that the rabbit's leg may not be broken, but the inventor of that trap could not have been a practical rabbit-catcher. It is not the hardness of the gin's jaws alone that breaks the rabbit's leg ; it is the rabbit itself that does the damage as it struggles to get free. Then a trap was tried which had long, curving jaws ; the idea being that the rabbit would be caught round the body instead of by a leg. That trap faded out. I never used one, but I suspect that the theory behind it was not borne out in practice. The rabbit is a cunning creature, and is not easily caught in any old contrivance. He can even evade the most skilfully set gin, if he has got some experience of it from watching his more unlucky brethren.

The wire snare is supposed, by the uninitiated, to be more humane than the steel gin, and certainly, if the poor rabbit had only sense enough to sit still as soon as the noose tightened, it would be a more humane method. But the rabbit does not sit still. He struggles frantically to get free, and the noose grows tighter and tighter round his neck until he can hardly breathe. If the rabbit struggles long enough, he is suffocated. That is the only humane part of rabbit snaring.

Rather strangely, a rabbit dies more quickly if the snare grips him in front of the ears instead of behind them. It is possible that the neck is dislocated when that occurs, but I have never proved that to my satisfaction. In any case, the wire snare cannot compete with the gin as an effective means of reducing rabbits. It will take off the cream, as one might say, but rabbits soon become very wary of it.

The long net, which is used along covert sides at night when rabbits are out feeding, is another method that can only catch a fraction of the stock. I have seldom used it, but keepers who have used it a lot tell me that good bags are sometimes made, if conditions are suitable. The darker and rougher the night the better are the chances of a good

haul with the long net, but rabbits have to be really numerous, and feeding a good way from the covert side. It is a
method greatly favoured by professional poachers, because
it is silent, and because there is only a short wait between
the setting of the net and the collecting of the booty. It is
also a comparatively painless method. No doubt, the
rabbits have a few moments of terror before someone slips
along the net in the darkness to draw their necks, but the
net itself inflicts no pain.

One of the great drawbacks of the long net, however, is
the fact that it can only be set in certain places. Over on
Swinside Fell, for instance, the long net is useless, because
the rabbit burrows are everywhere, and the rabbits feed
everywhere. The long net can only intercept rabbits as they
run back to their hiding places in a mass. Now and then,
it is used around exceptionally large burrows, when the
rabbits are bolted into it by ferrets, but that method is only
used rarely. It is easier to shoot the bolting rabbits than to
erect a cumbersome, hundred-yards-long net.

Bolting rabbits into purse nets, which are set at the
mouths of burrows, is another fairly good method of
getting rid of rabbits ; and if the burrows are dug every
time the ferret lies up, the efficacy of that method is increased, provided, of course, that there isn't much cover
nearby. Rabbits soon learn to lie out, if their burrows are
continually tainted with the smell of ferrets. Whether bolting to purse nets is a painless method depends on circumstances. One day rabbits may bolt freely as soon as the
ferret enters the burrow ; another day they refuse to budge.
Then the ferret proceeds to kill them leisurely ; or if it
cannot reach a vital part, it will scrape the fur from their
backs. Sometimes, after long torment, the rabbits decide
to bolt, and they are sorry-looking spectacles.

Shooting rabbits during the summer evenings when they
are out feeding is perhaps the most humane method of
killing rabbits, but it isn't much good if a drastic reduction
in their ranks is desired. And the weapon must be a shotgun.

The rifle can cause a lot of suffering even when used by an expert. Sooner or later a belly hit is registered, and the rabbit runs off apparently unharmed, only to die later in the burrow. It is easy to tell when a rabbit is hit in the wrong place by a bullet. There is a distinct plonk ! When I hear that, I am not glad. Nowadays, I seldom use the rifle on rabbits.

Poison gas I have never used. During the war there was great talk about this method of killing rabbits, but lately there has been little word of it. Probably it was not so effective as it promised to be. Certainly it could not deal with lying-out rabbits, nor could it reach the ones that lie snugly under river banks and in wayside drains. It might, however, kill the population of a large burrow more completely than anything else, but the food value of the destroyed rabbits would be lost, and that is something. Normally, part of a rabbit-catcher's wages is paid from the sale of his kill. And so we come back to the barbarous gin. It is in my opinion the best reducer of rabbits, if used by an expert, but I shall immediately throw it away when an effective, painless substitute appears.

Before I set gins anywhere, I usually form a plan. First of all I go to the scene of operations to find out exactly how many traps I need. Traps are heavy ; so that saves unnecessary labour. Then, if the ground is comparatively featureless, such as fellside ground often is, I set my traps after a certain system. In the first burrow I may put down four traps in a line ; in the next burrow I may put down three in the form of a triangle, then in the next burrow my traps may form roughly the figure T on the fellside, and so on. All that I remember, so that when I go to the traps again I can find them easily. If there are half a dozen traps or more in one burrow, I merely remember the number. By following that system I seldom lose a trap. As far as possible I try not to set odd traps here and there, because they often give trouble. Many an hour have I spent looking for odd traps. And it is important to find every trap, not because traps are valuable, but because humanity demands it. The lost trap nearly always catches something.

Of course, even the most conscientious trapper will lose a gin sometimes, especially after the first arrangement of his traps has been disturbed. He may decide, say, halfway through the week that all his gins aren't necessary where they were set on Monday ; so he lifts a few to set elsewhere. The trouble starts then. Unless he has an exceptionally good memory, he may find himself hunting hundreds of acres of country on Saturday morning for a missing trap. The best remedy for that is never to leave odd traps in widely-scattered burrows, but to lift one burrow clean, and leave another as it was set originally. The trapper has only to remember then that certain burrows which he set on Monday will be empty of traps on Saturday. So confusion is avoided.

One curious fact I have often noticed whilst trapping is that if I happen to be thinking hard about anything when I am setting a trap, the same thought will come to me the following day when I look for the trap. That has happened so often that I now accept it as commonplace. I may be thinking about something totally different when I go back to the trap, but sure enough the original thought will return. The same thing happens if I have been humming a tune whilst setting the trap. Next day I start humming the same tune at the same place. Apparently my mind has unconsciously taken in the configuration of the ground along with the thought or tune, and when the stimulus comes, so does the thought or tune. Very strange, indeed. And that happens even on bare fellsides where one burrow is almost like another.

Whether trapping is right or wrong is a moot point. Ask the farmer who is having trouble with rabbits, and he will probably say that any method is right if it rids him of a nuisance ; ask the ordinary person who has no crop to lose, and who is not held responsible for rabbit damage, and he will denounce the use of the gin strongly. Undoubtedly it is a cruel method, but it isn't easy, nor even possible to estimate a rabbit's capacity for suffering. Our human nervous system is more complex ; so our reaction and a rabbit's reaction to injury are two different sensations. I have seen a rabbit run away after losing a foot as if nothing were amiss. A man could not move with the same injury, and his life would be in danger if he got as little attention as the rabbit gets. Nevertheless, one ought to avoid giving pain to wild creatures, if that is at all possible.

Poor rabbits ! they are persecuted by many enemies. I have killed thousands myself, but I do not hate the creatures. On the contrary, I like to see them scuttling about the woodlands. It is only a pity that they don't have enough sense to know when they are arousing our ire. Actually they have as much right to the earth as we have, and they know nothing of title deeds. But they are a feeble folk, and must suffer for being feeble. Sometimes I do wish, though, that people would not vilify the rabbit, then ask for his flesh, because it ekes out their rations so admirably.

Moles

Mole destruction is not often included in a gamekeeper's duties. In fact, it is my experience that there are few game-keepers who understand fully the trapping of moles, al-though many gamekeepers can catch a mole in their gardens when the occasion demands. I learned the art as a boy ; so if the worst came, I could easily become a full-time mole-catcher.

Since the middle days of the war I have killed the moles in the woods and policies of this estate. I do not trap the farmlands. That is done by a local man who was appointed by the War Agricultural Executive Committee in the person of the pests officer for this district. He is paid by the farmers directly, and traps the land twice every winter as a rule. Payment is based on acreage. When this local mole-catcher was appointed, I was asked by our agent to kill the moles in these policies, which was a more convenient arrangement for the estate. I am always on the place, and can remove moles that get into the flower-beds and gardens any time.

The mole is a cunning animal. He has particularly keen scenting powers, and to trap him successfully, one must take certain precautions. For instance, the mole-catcher must not handle anything which has a strong, unusual smell immediately before he sets his traps. As an additional safeguard, he ought to rub his hands well with soil, so that there is as little human scent as possible on the traps.

I know that moles are caught sometimes in carelessly set traps, but more often they are found packed with earth, or pushed out of the run. When that happens, the mole has become educated, and even the most skilful trapper can hardly catch him then. But there are moles which have never had previous experience of a trap, yet they will not be caught. They display an amazing, natural sagacity. Each move that the trapper makes is defeated easily, until he is forced to give up in disgust, or to resort to poison. Even that may not be successful.

There are three main types of mole trap; the wooden barrel, the pincer, and what used to be known as the McPherson trap. The latter was evolved about Blairgowrie, Scotland, I believe, by a McPherson. It acts after the fashion of a mouse trap, now rarely seen, which was made of wood, and had several tunnels. A wire sprang up when the mouse touched the bait and pinned it to the roof of the tunnel. This mole trap which works on the same principle is a half-tunnel of galvanised metal. There is a loop of wire at each end. Two moles can, therefore, be caught in it. The loops are pulled upwards by springs, when the moles press forward the triggers. It is a light, handy trap, but better suited for grassland or heavy, clay land than loose, newly cultivated soil. That also applies to the pincer trap, which is made entirely of metal, and clutches the mole between the prongs, two of which are at each side of the trigger.

I prefer the wooden barrel trap, partly because I am used to it, and partly because it can be set easily in the lightest soil as well as in grassland. It is a slightly heavier trap than the others, especially after it has been set for some time in damp soil, and it is a little more troublesome to maintain than the others (it has two string loops that need renewal occasionally) but on the whole, I prefer it.

A lot of practice and observation are necessary before one can tell the difference between a mole run that is used almost daily and a gallery that has been driven by the mole whilst in search of food. One may catch a mole by setting the trap in a working tunnel, but days or weeks may elapse before success comes, and there is no guarantee that success will ever come ; so the efficient mole-catcher is the man who can sift the genuine run from a maze of false ones. The genuine run may not be got near the mole heaps at all. It may even be fifty or a hundred yards away. To the eye of the layman there may be nothing to indicate a good run, because the moles have used it for so many years that the original heaps have weathered away or become grown over with vegetation. Such old-established runs are often beneath a fence or alongside a stone wall. They are called 'highways' by mole-catchers, and amazing catches of moles are sometimes got in them. I don't know exactly why moles should use those highways that are often so far from any working heaps, but I suppose they have the wanderlust like many human beings ; and then they need water and, I suppose, some sleep. They obviously do not remain in the workings where they get their food all day. That is completely evident. If moles drove their galleries for worms until they were satisfied internally, and stopped about the same place until hunger made them work again, the mole-catcher would be compelled to set his traps among the heaps, and success would be rather erratic, but luckily, they go off some time every day for water or sleep or to see their friends.

But it must not be assumed that a mole-catcher who sets

his traps among the heaps is a dud. Sometimes there is no alternative. The run away from the heaps may not be visible even to the practised eye. It may be among bushes, or rank vegetation. Great skill is necessary then to find the true run among the heaps. I have found that a single run between two working areas often provides a kill ; and if the moles have gone to the trouble of making a run beneath a path or roadway, that is the place for a trap. Now and then I have been defeated in my search for the true run, especially among large workings along a river bank ; so I have put in a trap at each run that offered the least sign of success. Generally one trap would be in the right place.

When a particularly cunning mole defeats me repeatedly, I try some strategy. I will put perhaps a trap in the run at a different place, and I will choose a trap that has not been sprung for a week or more. In that manner I ensure that there is little, or no, human scent about it. And I will not touch the earth in the run with my bare hands. The spade and twigs will remove all the necessary soil. Despite all my care, I can never guarantee to kill a really cute mole, but I try and try again.

Poison is used a lot nowadays by mole-catchers, but more-so by those who work directly under pests officers. It is certainly a good method. Cunning moles may be destroyed by that means, when traps are useless ; but, of course, the exact quantity of moles killed is not known. Then the valuable skins are lost. Many a mole-catcher relies on the skins for a goodly part of his wages. And when all is said and done, the country loses a certain amount of wealth, if poison is exclusively used. Strychnine is the recognised poison for moles. It is a deadly substance, indeed, and requires careful handling. Some farmers object to its use on their land. They fear that their stock might suffer, but in the hands of a really careful man they need have little anxiety. Worms are used as bait, and no stock, except fowls and ducks, will lift worms. And when one considers that the worms are buried in the ground, the danger to poultry is lessened. Actually the greatest danger is to the man who uses strychnine. He cannot afford to be careless in his handling of it. A few crystals blown into his face on a windy day might end his career as a pests destroyer. He could easily achieve the same result if he handled poisoned worms, then ate his lunch without washing his hands thoroughly.

The procedure for poisoning moles is simple. If a big area has to be covered, the pests destroyer mixes as much strychnine as will lie comfortably on a sixpence with a two pound jam jar full of chopped worms. The poisoner does not need the same skill as the trapper. He can put his bait into a dozen runs, if he does not know where to find the true one. A mole will pass by eventually, with any luck at all. But moles are still numerous, despite all that is being done against them. As the Cumbrian puts it, there are yackers an' yackers aw upside down wid mowdies.

Foxes

In the Lake District fox can with truth be called the scourge of the countryside. He is an interesting animal, I admit, but an expensive luxury. Lambs have been worried every spring by foxes since I came to the hut. In some years the total has been considerable. Last spring they were serious. Several farmers around Keswick lost over thirty lambs, and nearly every fell flock was ravaged to some extent.

This spring reynard has been active again, but not to such a pitch as last year. Nevertheless, one Thornthwaite farmer was almost driven crazy by lamb losses. Every morning for over a fortnight he lost one. The hounds came and were cast off one Sunday morning in an endeavour to stop the nuisance. They ran a fox to Bassenthwaite, but the lambs continued to be killed. Then the farmer came to me. I felt that I could do very little, because the fox killed a fresh lamb each night, but I set a trap near Thornthwaite Birches. It was baited with the pitiful remains of a worried lamb. A carrion crow or two were all that it caught ; so I lifted the trap again, and the killer still roams the fells. If it had been coming back to its previous kills, one might have had some success. The farmer actually saw the fox eating a lamb one morning at daybreak, but he had no gun, otherwise he might have squared accounts with his enemy.

The various Lakeland packs of hounds kill a fair amount of foxes each year. But it is evident that they only keep them in check, as the bag is about the same each season, unless hard weather has stopped hunting over a long period. This year the bag will be smaller than usual, because the hounds were confined to kennel for months by the frost and deep snow.

When we had thousands of pheasants in these coverts, we were annoyed continually by foxes. Even although we killed them almost weekly, we could never say that we were nearing the end of our troubles. And the pheasants were not even safe when the shooting season was over. A fox once got into our laying pen near the Kennels, and killed seventy-odd birds one wild, wet night. The brute found where the wire-netting was joined, and had torn it open. How it got out again is still something of a mystery to me, as the netting had fallen together in such a manner that we only detected the place of entry with difficulty.

Every wild night during the shooting season, and even before the shooting season opened, there were deaths in the pheasant coverts from foxes. The birds were blown from their roosts in the young larch trees, and were unable to fly back again in the dark. Thus did reynard have a good time, if the storm happened to rise suddenly in the night. But if the storm happened to rage at dusk, we paraded the coverts with lanterns, firing blank cartridges every now and then. No doubt, we saved many a hundred pheasants by these precautions, but foxes contrived to get a bird here and there, despite the racket we made in the night. We found the remains of the tragedies for days after each storm. There would be perhaps a pair of wings at one place, the feathers clipped as if a pair of scissors had been used. At another place there would only be a few damp feathers scattered about and the gizzard somewhere nearby. At a third place the bird would be lying dead without any apparent mark on it. If, however, it were plucked, one would find two punctures at each side. Evidently the fox had been in a hurry to kill another bird, and had merely nipped that one and thrown it away. Many pheasants were killed in that wanton manner. When a fox finds plenty of easy victims, he will kill for the pleasure of killing. It is that wasteful habit which causes him to be disliked by gamekeepers. And the gamekeeper is to be forgiven if he tries by every means in his power to encompass the fox's death. Before my time here a hundred birds have been killed in one night by foxes. I have never been so unlucky, but I have had my vulpine troubles.

A fox can show great cunning in evading a trap, if he is suspicious that one is set for him. He will, if he is hungry, lift the bait from the side where there is no trap ; or, if that is not easy, he will spring it without being caught. But he will not as a rule reach for the bait again after the trap has snapped. He has convinced himself then that there is really danger and looks for something else. It is his keen nose that makes him difficult to catch ; but despite that, I have caught many a fox. I have also shot them at the end of an organised drive often, and on a few occasions I have got within range of them by chance.

One such lucky stroke occurred on a winter afternoon a few years ago. The grocer's boy had been up here to the hut with my rations, and was in the act of closing the door, when he pushed his head in again and said that a cat was making up into the wood. I stepped quickly to the door and was in time to see a fox disappear beneath the spruces on the bank. I grabbed my gun, hoping for a shot, but my hope was not very strong. The fox, I thought, must have been alarmed by the boy, and would probably make straight through the wood on to the open fell. But still, I decided to try for a shot. First I climbed the wood at the end in front of the hut, which was down-wind. I waited at an open place for nearly a quarter of an hour without seeing or hearing any sign of my enemy. Then I decided on an apparently foolish move. I came back along the front of the wood, and climbed it on the up-wind side. I was hoping that my scent would be confusing to the fox among the thick conifers and rhododendron bushes at that side. My hope was justified. As I came round a yew tree on the top, I saw the fox looking at me. He was standing beneath the oaks among some dead leaves. Without hesitation, I lifted my gun and fired. He rolled over, but gathered himself and tried to escape down into the thick conifers again, but he could not do it. I got up to him as he expired.

Another afternoon, a sunny one at that, and a Sunday, I saw a fox from my window standing a hundred yards in front of the hut on the greensward. I waited until he disappeared into the tall bracken, which was beginning to turn russet. As his brush vanished I got the gun and gave chase. At the edge of the bracken I stopped and scanned the wood as far as I could see into it, but he was not visible under the dark trees. Then I saw him quite suddenly against the fence. He was looking into the field, and was quite unaware of me. I was raising the gun carefully when he got behind a cherry tree and some reddish bracken, which confused me. In the sunlight the fox and the bracken were almost the same colour. A second later I was chagrined to see him slip up beneath the trees. If I had thought that he was going to get into the wood so easily, I might have risked a snap-shot, but I had expected to get an unobstructed view of my quarry ; so I held my fire until it was, as I thought, too late. The chances of getting on to even terms with the fox among thick trees on a quiet, sunny afternoon seemed remote. However, I waited a few seconds, and got quietly through the bracken. Luckily, there was a zig-zagging path up through the spruces at that precise place ; so I climbed it cautiously. Among the shadows between

me and the outside of the wood I saw a movement. Then
I saw the fox. He was gazing intently out towards the sunlight. Perhaps he had winded a rabbit. I could not tell that,
but I could see that something was interesting him. If he
had not been so interested, he might have seen me. I froze,
apprehensive that I might give my presence away by a
slight movement ; but in less than a minute the fox reluctantly turned his mask towards the inside of the wood,
and walked into a more open place above me. As he was
crossing the path I shot him dead. He was a big dog fox.
Why he should be wandering about on a sunny afternoon I
cannot say, but he paid the penalty for his rashness.

Last spring I got one over on Swinside Fell rather
luckily. Jim Bainbridge over at Swinside Cottages had been
losing hens. He was in despair. The hens lived in a little
house at the foot of Swinside Crag, a place where reynard
could reach them without his being seen easily. I scoured
the fell, but saw neither fox nor sign of cubs. Still the
depredations continued. Then the two Swainson brothers,
Eardly and Morris, who rent the fell, found evidence of
cubs. I came on them one evening about nine o'clock
digging an earth, which had been enlarged from a rabbit
burrow. They had broken into it at several places, but
could not find the cubs. The vixen appeared on the fellside
above them while they were digging ; so they were fairly
certain that the cubs were still inside. Finally I went to the
wood near Derwentwater for some traps, which I set, but
I had little hope of catching anything after the disturbance
we had made about the earth. Next morning, Tuesday, there
was nothing in the traps, nor had anything touched them.
On Wednesday morning a trap was sprung, but nothing
was in it. On Saturday morning I got a cub ; so I left the
traps sitting. A few days later I got another, and that was
all. The rest of the litter had been in the earth the whole
time ; but one night the vixen burrowed right down without
going near an entrance, and took them away. That did not
gladden me, because I knew that there might still be

trouble among poultry or lambs, if a new foxy home were established on the fell.

Now, one morning a week later I had some time to spare before I collected my pay. I decided to utilize it in climbing the fell, not with the sole intention of trying to locate the cubs again, but merely to see what there might be in the way of vermin up there in the larch plantations.

I fired at a jay, without effect, in the top plantation, then I got out on to the highridge. The summit was about a couple of hundred yards from me and perhaps a hundred feet higher; so I walked round it to see what was doing on the Newlands Valley side. The wind was blowing in my face. As Causey Pike began to appear across the dale in front of me, I looked to my right down the fellside and saw a fox wandering aimlessly on a piece of open ground. Immediately, I dropped into the short heather, which I was traversing, and did not even try to see where the fox was going. Too often have I seen foxes escape by a slight movement of the hunter. A few minutes later, from the corner of my right eye, I saw the fox trotting along a sheep track below me, and towards me. When she got to the nearest point on the track, long shot though it was, I swung my gun round and gave her the right barrel. She gathered herself together, and bounded forward; so without hurry, I fired my left. That drew her up. She was visibly hard hit, but I pushed another cartridge into the choke and laid her dead among the russet bracken. She proved to be the mother of the cubs; so there were no more hens worried, and the lambs were saved from a potential menace. I took the vixen down to Jim Bainbridge to show him definitely that his poultry was safe, for a time, at least.

Foxes can be ghoulish creatures. A little over a year ago one started to dig into the grave of my old labrador bitch, Peggy, which is under a larch tree over at the edge of the wood, about seventy yards from the hut. I filled in the scrapings, but a few nights later the grave was opened again more completely, and part of the body eaten. That did not please me at all ; so I set a trap carefully after I had improved the runway. Unfortunately, there was a severe frost that night, which must have interfered with the working of the trap, because it was sprung empty next morning. However, the fox took the hint and left Peggy's resting place alone.

One morning a week or two later, as I was climbing through some thinly-scattered spruces along the wood, I saw a fox in front of me. He made off, keeping a tree between himself and me all the time, as far as he was able. That is a trick, by the way, that most hunted creatures have. But the half-grown spruce was not thick enough to give him full protection. I fired through the branches, then I fired again as he was climbing a crag in the open. I did not pick him, and I suppose that he got on to the fell eventually, but whether he lived or died, Peggy's grave was left in peace ever after.

Often in the winter evenings a year ago I saw a fox on the fell-end straight above the hut. Never could I get a shot at him, although I tried hard. Once I saw him chase a rabbit. I was just over the wall in the wood, and my attention was drawn to the fellside by a rustling of dead bracken. I flopped on my stomach, hoping that he had not seen me. Vain hope ! When I looked again, he was silhouetted on the highridge. He stood immobile for several minutes, for so long, in fact, that I began to wonder if I were really looking at the fox. then he bounded up the highridge, and disappeared.

Several weeks later, two months perhaps, I was coming up the lonning from the village in the gloaming. I heard a fox bark on the fell-end above Relph's farm, and as I had my gun with me, I made in the direction of the fox. When I got into Relph's garth, I stopped to listen for another bark. A village youth and his girl friend came past on the path that goes over the fell-end behind the wood to Newlands ; so I asked if they had heard any barking. They said that not only had they heard the bark, but that the fox

E

had barked at them. A few days later some cubs were found near there, which seemed to indicate that the fox had been going to them, and had resented the presence of human beings in the neighbourhood. Or she may have been annoyed that her hunting was being interfered with. Whatever was her reason matters little. It was a unique incident. I have never known of another fox that would deliberately bark at human beings, although I have known foxes appear when people were trying to get their cubs out of an earth. One would think that that would be provocation enough to make a fox bark.

When foxes have got the blood-lust on them, they are often blind to some extent to the danger that they themselves are running, but they generally manage to curb their appetite for killing before they themselves are killed ; that is, of course, if they get a fair chance. But one fox that I remember was so desperately intent on murder that he lost temporarily his fear of man. The man in this case was I. My pheasant-rearing fields at the time were between this wood and the thick spruce wood down near the beckside. It was a stormy, wet day, and I had delayed the one o'clock feed, in the hope that the weather would become better. About two o'clock I decided that the pheasant chicks, which were then about a month old, could wait no longer ; so I put on a coat, grabbed my bucket, and started to feed. Before I had got to the end of the first row, I heard the hens cackling down near the wood. The sound only came faintly to me, as it was blowing furiously, and rain was drifting over the fields. I set down my bucket and went to investigate the disturbance. Visibility was bad, and the backs of the coops were towards me ; so I could not see which hens were alarmed. Just as I got through the gateway into the bottom field, I saw a fox chasing birds about eighty yards away. I sprinted as hard as I was able towards it down the diagonal path that led from the gateway to the gap in the wood, which gave access to the beckside. The fox must have seen me, but came determinedly in my direction after a pheasant chick. In fact it got so near to me that I aimed a kick at its head. Unfortunately, I missed by about a foot ; then it turned and made into the wood. I did not expect to see it again, but I rushed through the gap, and got over the wooden bridge to the far side of the beck, where there was a feed hut. In that hut were two guns and an old man, who was a general help during the rearing season. I took the double-barrelled gun and the old man took the single, although he had hardly ever fired a shot in his life, and we made over the bridge to the gap in the wood. The hens nearest the wood were making a tre- mendous racket as we got there, but we could not see them for the trees, and I thought that they had not got over their first scare. When we looked through the gap, however, we knew differently. The fox was hard at work again. He was in the act of grabbing a fluttering bird as I lifted my gun, and even when I shot the forelegs from under it, the desperate creature lunged forward and snapped at the chick. It was an incredible action. The bird escaped into a little heap of branches, and the fox tried to wriggle somehow back into the cover. I gave it the second barrel, and the old man gave it a shot also in his excitement, which put an end to its career. We picked up nine dead chicks. Actually, I was fortunate. If I had fed my birds at the usual time, and gone back to change my wet clothes, the fox might easily have killed half of the birds in that field. The amazing part of the incident was that the fox came back after I had literally chased it off the field. When I went for the gun, I hoped that I might see the fox leave the wood somewhere, or that the old man might drive it out to me, but I never dreamed that it would return to its killing in broad daylight. Which shows that every fox is not always frightened by the presence of man.

It is fairly evident that foxes visit all the henhouses in their locality almost every night. That is amply proved in the Lake District ; for if any henhouse is left unfastened only once, and foxes can reach it, there is a sad tale to tell

in the morning. Often there is nothing left but a few
feathers. Occasionally a bird is found buried here and
there, but nothing like the original numbers are ever
accounted for. Foxes will often carry their victims for
miles. I have seen poultry feathers far back among the
Derwent Fells, nowhere near a henhouse.

Writing of henhouses, reminds me of an impudent fox,
which was operating up the dale about two years ago at the
mouth of Smeltmill Ghyll. The first time that I saw it I was
climbing up Rowling End on the far side of the ghyll one
evening at dusk. I was looking for a rabbit, and was, therefore, advancing cautiously up to an outcrop of rock,
hoping that something might be sitting within shooting
range when I got near enough to it to look over. A rabbit
was there, but, unluckily, it saw me first and bolted without
a shot. Then I turned to look down into the ghyll, and saw
a fox running hard towards the road, which it reached at
the point almost where I had left it a few minutes before to
climb the fell. It crossed the road and disappeared over the
steep bank at the far side, but it did not jump over the wall,
because I could see the top of the wall, although the bottom
was hidden from me. Obviously it had gone along the wall
side towards the bêck, and was just as obviously making
for Stoneycroft poultry farm across the beck. That the
fox had seen me I had not the slightest doubt, otherwise it
would not have been running so hard. At the time I did
not stop to weigh the pros and cons of the matter. As soon
as the fox vanished over the bank I bolted as hard as I was
able down the fellside after it. There was the faint chance of a
shot if it wasted any time by the wall. When I looked over
the bank, however, the fox was nowhere visible ; so I
walked towards the bridge, keeping a sharp lookout as I
did so towards Stoneycroft on the steepish ground opposite. On the higher side of the road from Stoneycroft
farm-house is a triangular meadow. It lies right up to the
mouth of the ghyll, and that evening there were several
poultry arks in it. At one ark the hens were standing about

aimlessly before they retired for the night. The light was
failing, but the hens were quite distinct, because they were
white leghorns. As I stood by the bridge, I saw the fox
making up that meadow. If it had carried on in a straight
line, it would have passed to the left of the hens, and missed
them by perhaps a score of yards. But when it got abreast
of them, it made a sudden rush to the right and grabbed a
fowl. The rest of the hens scattered in alarm, and the fox,
carrying its victim, went through the wire fence on to
Barrow Fell, which is at the Stoneycroft side of the ghyll.
I was astonished for a second or two, then more in anger
than expectation of doing the fox any harm at a range of
about a hundred and fifty yards, I fired my gun at it as it
climbed the fellside. It dropped the fowl, rather surprisingly.
I saw the poor creature roll down the slope among the
russet bracken for half a dozen yards, but reynard was not
inclined to let the booty go so easily. It rushed after the
hen, retrieved it quickly, and vanished over the shoulder
of the fell into Smeltmill Ghyll. Just then the poultry
farmer, Mr. Whitson, came out from his house on to the
road. He shouted down to me, and asked what I was
shooting at. I bawled back the gist of the incident, which
apparently surprised him, as he had neither seen the fox
nor heard the commotion among his fowls. But he was
quite convinced that a fox had actually been there, when
we went up the meadow. White feathers were scattered on
the grass, and when he counted the hens, one was absent.
All that happened on a Wednesday evening.

Now, I imagined that it was merely an isolated incident,
an example of foxy barefacedness that would not occur
readily again, and I thought little more of the affair. But two
evenings later two hens were taken away in broad daylight.
The farmer's wife saw one go, and she tried to scare the
fox by making a noise, but reynard refused to be scared.
The cunning brute knew that a racket signified some degree
of safety. Miss Robinson, of Stair Mill, a house a hundred
yards down the beckside from Stoneycroft, saw the second

hen go. Mr. Whitson became perturbed then. He came to me to see what I could do to stop the nuisance ; so an hour before dusk on the Saturday evening I went along to Stoneycroft, and hid myself in a depression on the fellside above the triangular meadow. Through the fence, and about thirty yards on my left, was the ark, which had been subject to the fox's attentions. One difference, however, was that there were sheep in the field. I saw that if the fox came I would have to shoot at it before it got into the field, otherwise the sheep might be in my line of fire at the critical moment. The fox would assuredly see to that. So, I got down among the russet bracken. The new fronds were just appearing, but they were too short either to obstruct my view, or to hide me. In any case, the depression afforded me all the shelter that I needed. Beside the ark the hens were moping about as all hens mope about before they finally retire. At twenty minutes to ten the fox appeared without any warning by the wire fence. It was about forty yards off, and was peering intently at the hens, which were quite unaware of its presence. The brute seemed to be choosing a victim. Forty yards was a long shot for ordinary game ammunition (I was loaded with No. 5) but there was little possibility of a nearer one ; so I pushed forward my gun and fired. The fox, a big one, reeled and almost fell as the charge struck it, but gathered itself and sprang on to the fell. I was on my feet in an instant and gave it the second barrel, without, however, stopping it. As it neared the shoulder of the fell, I fired a parting shot, and that was the last I saw of it. I scoured the ghyll for a few hundred yards back, hoping to pick up reynard dead, but there was no sign. Before I made back to the hut, I had a look at the place where the fox had been standing. A fencing post had been hit by some pellets, and I was satisfied that the cartridge had not lacked power. Some splinters of wood told me that. So that nuisance was ended. I have an idea that there were cubs somewhere up the ghyll, or behind Barrow, but although I searched, I could not find them.

Foxes come quite near to the hut sometimes. I have seen their tracks only twenty yards away in the snow. One dark night my grocer saw a fox by the light of his electric torch below the big cherry tree behind the hut. Once I trapped one only thirty yards from the hut, and this week I shot at a fox from my bedroom window. I did not pick it up, but it left some fur behind ; so it certainly was hit hard.

I shot at the fox on Thursday morning, but I first saw the brute at a quarter to seven on Tuesday. When I got up I looked through the open bedroom window, and was surprised to see no rabbits feeding. Usually I see three at least between the hut and the wood. I was in the act of lighting the fire. As I reached for the matches, I turned and looked through the kitchen window. A fox was standing immobile about fifty yards away on the middle of the glade. It was looking intently at some young rabbits that have been bred in a small burrow there. The rabbits went underground, and the fox, finding nothing further to interest it, went leisurely up to the wood and disappeared under the spruces and firs. I got the gun and tried to intercept it at the top, but I heard three carrion crows making a fearful racket up on the fell ; so I surmised that the fox had gone right through the wood without stopping after I saw it last. And that was all for Tuesday.

On Thursday morning at 6.25 I was lying awake. A blackbird uttered its warning pipe up at the edge of the wood ; so I got up and looked through the open window, but I kept well back. A fox was standing fifty yards away under a Scots fir. Later I discovered that it had been eating a young rabbit, but at that time it appeared merely to be looking in the direction of the hut. I slipped through to the kitchen for my gun, inserted two cartridges into the chambers, and came back quietly into the bedroom. My bedroom door sometimes squeaks, but fortunately it was silent that morning. I aligned the gun without delay, for I know how precious time is when dealing with those creatures, and I fired. There was a terrific detonation in the bedroom, and the fox ran at right angles to me and to my left. It got the other barrel, which made it visibly stumble, but it turned then and ran up into the wood. Since that morning I have seen no young rabbits up there under the trees. No doubt, the fox killed the lot. The one which I picked up more than half eaten appeared to be barely a month old. The old rabbits have been out feeding every morning since then; so I have given reynard something to consider, if I have not killed him.

One Sunday morning about a couple of years ago I might have shot a fox dead from my bedroom window, if the gun had been at hand. It was near enough when I saw it first. I was awake, and heard a rabbit scream. The scream died away to a piteous wail. I got up, looked towards the wood, but saw nothing. Then, with the corner of my right eye, I saw a fox making up towards the bracken, which was tall then, with a half-grown rabbit in its jaws. It paused a second before it entered, then the dewy bracken closed over it. If I had rushed through for the gun when I heard the first squeal, instead of gazing through the window, I daresay that I might have got the fox, but I thought that the tragedy was being enacted up under the trees.

In the pheasant-rearing days here we had fox drives in the woods and occasionally on the fells. The fox-hunting people did not look with much favour on these drives, but their sport actually suffered nothing at all. There were always plenty of foxes for the hounds. Often there were too many. The hounds would put up one fox, hunt it for half an hour, then raise another and another, until they were completely baffled by a multiplicity of scents. That sort of confusion occurs yet. When the hounds cast off on Barrow for the first time last autumn, about half a dozen foxes were being hunted at the same time. Two came through this wood, and jumped the fence at the end nearest to the village. I saw another go down the meadows into the beckside wood, and several were being hunted at the same time on the fell. One was finally killed, but it had to be bolted twice from rabbit holes along beyond the screes above Uzzicar Farm.

Stillness and silence are essential to success, when one is waiting at the receiving end of a fox drive. Foxes can spot the fidgety person a long way off, and they are quick to hear the slightest noise. They can also act very swiftly, if they get the least whiff of human scent. I once proved that quite conclusively when the high plantation on Swinside Fell was being driven to another gun and me. We made a detour from the top of the fell to get into our positions at the lower end, but a crag compelled us to walk for a few yards by the plantation fence. These few yards that we walked by the fence saved a fox's life. I was lying behind an outcrop of rock twenty yards from the corner post of the fence, expecting the fox to leap over the wire-netting into the open, when I saw it trotting down by the fence towards me. I felt certain that I would get it, and remained immobile until my quarry got nearer. On the fox came, quite unsuspicious, I thought, but when it reached the place where we had gone by the plantation edge, it leapt without hesitation over the fence, and was lost among the young trees. That was the last I or anybody else saw of it that day. Another fox met its end rather unluckily in the vicinity of that same plantation. I suppose all foxes are unlucky if they meet their end while still in their prime, but this fox was unluckier than usual. We had decided to drive the plantation one morning, as a fox had been killing pheasants in that quarter for a few days.

I had some rabbit traps set on the fell top, which I looked before I went to meet the other guns and beaters. As I came under the plantation to get to my destination, I saw a fox enter it, but whether the creature saw me or not I could not tell. It was some distance from me ; so I had done nothing unusual to alarm it. Then I met the gang of guns and beaters, and told them that there was a fox in the cover. The beaters, who were estate men, climbed the fell to get to the top of the plantation and found what was almost certainly the same fox in one of the rabbit traps that I had seen empty half an hour previously. They killed it, and that was the bag for the day. It is the only fox that ever got caught in my rabbit traps in full daylight.

A dale farmer once told me that in a long life of shepherding he had never put up a fox on the fell. His sheep ran on Catbells, which is perhaps not the best place for finding a fox, but still, it seems remarkable to me that a man could spend a lifetime among those fox-infested fells without once putting a fox off its lair. In fact, his admission was so remarkable that I could not believe it. Undoubtedly, he had never seen a fox rise at his approach, but I am quite certain that he had risen scores, and never caught a glimpse of them. Foxes can slip away very unobtrusively sometimes. They make use of every little bit of cover. I have seen them vanish into shallow gullies, and never appear again. Yet it was impossible to tell how they had got out without being seen.

When the hounds draw a fellside, they almost invariably put off a fox, but if a man were to walk across the same ground he might think that there were no foxes within miles of him, unless he happened by chance to be looking far ahead. Then he might get a glimpse of a red form slipping away through the ling. It is not often that I have put a fox up near enough to get a shot at it, but I have occasionally seen one in the distance as it made off in front of me.

My first experience of a fox after I came to the Lake District was on Rowling End. I was ferreting the face above the farm of the same name, and my ferret decided to lie up. It was a big, deep burrow; so I did not dig. An hour passed without any sign of the ferret, and to keep myself warm I climbed the fell as far as the ling. A fox rose forty yards or so above me. It presented its right side to me for a few yards; so I gave it a couple of barrels. On it went, however, and disappeared. A week later we found a fox lying dead on Swinside Fell with a damaged right foreleg. Obviously it was the same fox. It had travelled a mile, and crossed the dale, before it had expired.

One sunny, windy afternoon last spring, I surprised a fox

on Barrow Fell. I was on the fell looking at some rabbit
burrows between the screes, and I got a hunch that I would
see a fox, if I climbed up to the rough ling. There was
nothing supernatural about the hunch. Most of the ling
had been burned from the front of the fell, and the ling
above me was almost the only cover on this side. I, therefore, made my way cautiously through the thick, rough
cover, which was on a slope nearly as steep as the roof of a
house, when I saw the top of a fox's head above the ling.
The fox was looking in my direction, and I felt certain that
it had winded me, because the breeze was, unluckily and
unusually, blowing uphill. It was about seventy yards off ;
so I dropped on my stomach, and wriggled upwards,
hoping all the time that curiosity would make the fox stay
until I got a little nearer. I was disappointed. There was a
momentary flash of red between two clumps of ling, which
indicated to me that reynard was off. However, I wriggled
upwards steadily and without noise. Suddenly, the fox's
head and foreparts appeared above me again about forty
yards off. I raised my gun swiftly, and fired the choke
barrel. The fox vanished immediately. I climbed up as fast
as I could, which was not very fast, but there was no sign
of my quarry. I searched about in the tall ling for ten
minutes or so, then I went down to the place where I had
first seen the fox. There I found half of a freshly-killed rabbit.
The head was lying a yard from it. Evidently I had disturbed the fox at a meal, which explained why it had
showed itself a second time. Of course, if I had really
alarmed it the first time, it would have been over the hills
and far away, meal or no meal.

After I had convinced myself that the fox was not lying
dead on this side of the fell, I went over the highridge into
the Coledale side. I searched some heather there without
success, then I headed towards Barrowdores, which is the
gap between Barrow and Steel Point. Causey Pike on the
other side of Smeltmill Ghyll fills the gap, as one advances
through the Coledale slope of Barrow. There is a lot of

rough, craggy fell up at Barrowdores, which I thought might be the hiding place for another fox. I got through the fell breast without seeing anything, and on to the sheep track, which would lead me to the top of the rocks where I hoped to find reynard, when an extra stiff gust of wind made me stumble on the stony track. I fell forward, but I did not fall far, because the ground there was very steep. Nevertheless, those few seconds of inattention to the job in hand saved a fox's life. When I got upright, I saw a big fox below me, and slightly behind me, going over the heather in great bounds. I cocked my gun rapidly, slewed round to my right, and fired a shot after him as he disappeared into a shallow gully that ran down to the beck. A moment or two later it appeared at the beck, and started to climb the slope of Steel Point on the opposite side. Fifty yards up from the beck it stopped, which seemed to indicate that my shot had taken some effect, then it continued and vanished over the shoulder of the fell. The rattling of the stones, when I stumbled, had warned the creature of my proximity, and my short inattention had enabled it to get out of effective gunshot. So I rose two foxes in one afternoon, and with any luck I might have shot both.

Mr. Whitson, the poultry farmer along at Stoneycroft, came to me last year with a story of a fox, which was wandering about among his hens in broad daylight, even in brilliant sunshine. It had grabbed several hens, but one or two had escaped, because the poultry women had scared it off. I went along with the gun on several successive evenings and afternoons, but was not lucky enough to see the raider. It seemed to me to be a queerish fox, and I suspected that it was either a mangy one, or a big cub. The fox continued to be a nuisance ; so Mr. Whitson decided to call in the pests officer to see if he could arrange a drive on the fell. I told him that the fox was probably not living on the fell, in fact, a nearby cornfield, which was nearly ripe, seemed a more likely place. But nevertheless, the pests officer arrived one evening. He called at the hut on his way up the dale, but finding that I was not at home, he carried on and overtook me near the fell gate at the up-dale end of this wood. He stopped his car and we had a talk about the fox, and the uselessness of driving a vast area of bracken-covered fell. Then he left me, and went on to see Mr. Whitson. That same evening, I set a trap, baited with a piece of rabbit, at a place where I thought the fox might pass on its way to the hens. I could not set it among the poultry-houses, otherwise I might have done more damage than the fox. Next morning I looked the trap early, and finding nothing in it, I put a flat slab of stone over the plate. I intended to take the piece of stone off the trap again that evening and try for the fox without having to set the trap up afresh. The less human scent there is about a trap the better.

When I had made the trap safe for poultry and dogs, I went over to feed my ferrets at the Kennels. Coming back, I met one of the Stoneycroft poultry women on the road. It was apparently her day off. She congratulated me on my success with the trap. I was stupefied. There had been no fox in the trap, and I knew that no one could have taken a fox out of the trap and set it up without my knowledge ; so I asked the woman what fox she was talking about. Then she told me that another poultry woman had picked up a nearly-full-grown fox cub underneath one of her houses that morning. It was dead, and the cause of its death was evidently a wound in one of the hind legs, which had been caused by a trap. I was more than ever mystified, but I went straightaway across to Stoneycroft, and asked the poultry woman, a Land Army girl, to produce the fox cub. It had a bad hind leg, without any doubt, but it was green with gangrene or something as bad, and the original wound could not possibly have been caused by a trap. Then I remembered that the dogs at Uzzicar Farm, which adjoins Stoneycroft, had worried a cub not long before that, but the cub had escaped. Quite evidently the cub had lost its mother somehow, and had been forced at an early age to fend for itself. Hence the boldness. I am certain that it had never been far from the poultry-houses for weeks, and it might have done a lot of damage, if those dogs had not set on it one day beside Uzzicar farmhouse. I was thankful to learn of its demise. Mr. Whitson was even more thankful.

Mangy foxes have a habit of skulking about in daylight looking for easy prey, but it's a long time now since I saw one of those repulsive creatures. Once on Swinside Fell I got one which had practically no fur whatever on it. Another which was shot near the Kennels was almost as bad. Jock Stark shot that one at his back door in a ditch. It had been seen often by estate men before it met its end.

It is not often that a fox will venture into a building, unless it is hotly pursued by hounds. During the recent heavy snow, however, a fox went into an outbuilding at Braithwaite Lodge to eat a rabbit. Charlie Relph, the farmer, told me about the incident. He was having a last look round his stock that night, and saw some fox tracks in the snow. He followed them to an implement shed, where they disappeared under the door, which is raised perhaps a foot from the ground. There were no tracks leaving the shed; so Charlie surmised that the fox was inside, but he could do nothing to get hold of it. The gap was too big to stop up with anything handy, and the fox would probably not have waited until he got a gun. When he opened the door, reynard darted past him. In the morning he found a partly-eaten rabbit in a corner. It is extremely unlikely that the fox killed the rabbit on the fell or in the field nearby and took it into the shed to eat. More probably the rabbit was already inside looking for food. The snow had been lying for weeks, and wild creatures were becoming desperate.

A dalesman told me once of a fox which was even bolder than the one at Charlie Relph's, although it did not actually enter a building. He and another shepherd were doctoring some sheep in an outbuilding one winter night by the light of a hurricane lamp. A hen was roosting in the window, which was without glass. Suddenly there was a squawking and flapping, and they saw a fox vanish into the darkness with the luckless fowl. That was, indeed, an impudent fox.

Reynard is bad enough, I know, but sometimes he is blamed unjustly. A few years ago a lot of hens were lost at various places around here. Feathers were usually found strewn about the hen-houses, and even entrails occasionally. Foxes were blamed. Then some sharp fellow noticed the imprint of a hobnailed boot where a 'fox' had been operating. The police became interested then, and the depredations ceased.

Cats

There are no true wild cats in the Lake District, but there are plenty of domestic cats that have gone wild. They are a nuisance among game and song birds, and may become almost as truly wild as their brethren in the Highlands of Scotland. I have seen them bolt for cover when they have been no nearer to me than a hundred yards, and they take advantage of every possible concealment just as skilfully as a fox does. But for every pariah there are scores of cats that lead a dual existence. By day they appear to be innocent, tame creatures ; by night they may go an incredible distance in search of prey. A mile is quite a possible distance for a poaching cat to travel in a night.

The owners often know nothing of those nocturnal forays, or, at least, they often appear not to know, but if the cat fails to appear some morning, the nearest keeper is usually blamed for its non-appearance. Where there is toothsome, easy prey there will always be cats to hunt it. That is a fact. The amount of cats that live on the country is surprising. No sooner is one feline removed than another takes its place.

A cat's work among rabbits is easily recognised. The forepart is always eaten first, but the head is left. When the meal is finished, the remainder of the rabbit is usually covered with grass or rubbish of some sort ; for a cat generally returns to its kill. That makes it easier than some other animals to trap. But it must not be inferred that a cat will step into any badly-set trap just because it has lived with human beings. Some cats are more wary than others, but the wide-awake ones can compete with the fox for astuteness. And I have known cats that could compete with him for rapacity.

One cat that I particularly remember wreaked so much havoc among my snares that I actually thought that I was being pestered by a fox. Several times I had set snares along a fence that runs up to the stone wall at the foot of Barrow Fell, but always I was compelled to lift them after a couple of nights or so, as most of the rabbits were being torn out. The rabbits were not merely eaten into, and the remaining portion covered with a wisp of grass. That would have signified a cat's work to me at once. Instead, the rabbits were torn out completely ; or only the head was left, if the snare happened to be an unusually strong one. Obviously, it was the work of a heavy animal. I set a trap. It was sprung empty the first night ; so, discouraged, I let a week elapse before I tried again. It was not possible to leave the trap set indefinitely in such a place, as the farmer's dog, or somebody else's dog, might have got into it. And in any case, sheep might have been turned into the field at any time.

After another night of destruction I set the trap again. I was as careful over the setting of it as if I were trying to catch the wariest fox in Lakeland. About ten o'clock at night I decided to go along to see whether anything had stepped into the trap. There was no moon, but the night was quite luminous. Before I got to the scene of operations I heard the wire fence rattling. Something was caught, and the something was fairly powerful. I thought that only a big dog fox could have made such a commotion, but I was astonished, when I got closer, to see that the trap had caught an enormous cat. Without exception it was the biggest cat I had ever seen. That ended the nuisance there.

I do not remember any trouble with cats in my rearing-fields, except once ; and the pheasant coops were so near to the house where the cats lived that there was a certain amount of excuse for their depredations. When I discovered that my birds were dwindling in the coops nearest to the garden hedge, I drew them farther into the field, so that the young pheasants were less likely to stray into the danger zone. I saved a lot of birds by taking that precaution, but occasionally at dusk I saw the marauders slinking along the field side of the hedge, hoping, I suppose, that I would not see them. They knew perfectly well that they were guilty, because they made off home with great bounds, if they saw me advance with the gun in a menacing position.

When the pheasants were taken to the woods, however, I sometimes had trouble with cats. There were generally a few coops in front of the hut, and one evening about eight o'clock I saw a cat come up the path. I watched it from the window, and I decided that I would let it go unmolested, if it showed no desire to attack a pheasant. There are cats that will not readily kill a pheasant, although they may be merciless hunters of fur. On came the cat that evening towards the hut. Now and then it stopped to scan the rough grass at the side of the path. Suddenly it became rigid. A half-grown pheasant was searching for insects, quite unaware of danger, about three yards from the cat, which seemed to be planning its attack.

I got my gun and slipped in a couple of cartridges. The cat moved towards its victim with legs as stiff as stilts. There was no sign whatever of a crouch. When it got to within four feet of the still unsuspecting pheasant, it paused for five seconds, then it hurled itself as from a catapult on to the bird's back. I saw them roll over as one, and decided the time for my intervention was more than ripe. Out through the doorway I darted, and down the path until I was twenty yards from the struggling creatures. When I got a good chance, I fired. The cat rolled over dead, but the pheasant, rather surprisingly, flew off among the trees. I expected to pick up the pheasant dead sometime the following day, but, as far as I could tell, it did not die from the effects of that adventure. Probably it had been covered by the cat when I fired.

I am convinced that the feral nature is not greatly subdued even in the tamest cat. When I go to the Kennels with a bagful of rabbits, a cat from one of the cottages nearby comes to me for tit-bits. It is the most affectionate cat on earth. It follows me about like a dog. It is clever. It knows when it is doing wrong. Sometimes I leave rabbits on a stone table near the game-larder while I attend to the ferrets. In my absence the cat will often jump on to the table, but immediately I appear, it leaps on to the ground guiltily. Altogether it is a superior cat, but watch it craftily stalking a robin, and the old Adam is apparent. Or throw down a rabbit in front of it, and watch it dig all four sets of claws into the dead body, as if it were still in the jungle and had just killed its prey.

That cat came home one morning from its covert-hunting in a sorry state. It had scratches on its face, and several marks which looked like fang punctures on one foreleg. Evidently it had met some hostile animal in its travels. I wondered whether a fox were responsible for its condition. I know that a fox will dig up the carcase of any semi-wild cat that has been buried in the coverts, but I do not know what would happen if the fox met the cat alive. It was quite evident, however, that this cat had been in a battle. In addition to the punctures and scratches, its fur was wet and it had a listless air, which was foreign to its usual vital appearance.

Stoats

At one time I could push a bare trap into any stone wall, or among stones by a beckside, and in a few days a stoat would be caught. No so today. Stoats have dwindled among these fells in recent years, but they have not been reduced by human contrivances. They may have been decimated by disease, but it is much more likely that the great increase in the fox population has some connection with the disappearance of stoats, because I have never seen dead stoats lying about the woods and fellsides. If disease had ever been rife, I feel certain that I would have seen signs of it somewhere. At the same time, I would hardly say that stoats were in danger of extinction in the Lake District yet. Every now and then I come across one of those agile marauders in my travels.

Not everybody knows that the stoat can climb a tree or bush with as much agility as a squirrel. I have shot many a stoat high in a bush, but I have never seen one, say, fifty feet from the ground in a tree. I do not doubt that a stoat could climb that height, but apparently he only goes high enough to find fledgling birds or eggs. He is a fast worker. I have watched him hunt a hedge. He skips along the ground for a few yards, then in a flash he is among the topmost branches. Down he comes again and repeats the manoeuvre. While he is occupied with his nefarious schemes the parent birds follow him with a tremendous chattering, but he pays not the slightest heed to them. Nevertheless, that chattering has been the indirect death of many a stoat. The keeper pushes off the safety catch of his gun when he hears it. But probably the blackbird's warning pipe has brought death to more stoats than the note of any other bird in the covert. It is a sure announcement that some four-footed marauder is astir. The chatterers may possibly be mobbing a jay or an owl, but that ominous pipe always follows a predatory animal.

Once in Swinside Moss, before it was felled, the chirping of a hen pheasant brought me to the scene of a tragedy. It was a sunny, summer morning. I stalked carefully along the dappled ride in the direction of the distress signals with my gun at the ready. Below a fir tree I saw a hen pheasant standing with her neck craned. Every few seconds she chirped, and all the time she kept looking fixedly at a clump of bramble cover nearby. Then I saw some lithe, brown things vanish into a rabbit burrow beneath a spruce. I remained still, and in a moment or two a young stoat appeared at the mouth of a hole ; so I shot it. Finally I got two more. While I was standing, a tiny, week-old chick went cheeping out of the grass to its mother. She walked off a few yards with it, calling frequently, but no other chick appeared. The stoats had done their vile work well. I found the rest of the brood, seven or eight chicks, lying about the ride dead.

There were some traps quite near ; so I got them, and set one in each entrance to the burrow. In a day I got the whole family of stoats. There were six young ones and the old bitch. It was here in front of the hut that I once saw a stoat go through the most extraordinary contortions. He was trying to get hold of a half-grown pheasant, and was so persevering and artful that he almost deserved to win.

My attention was drawn by the seven or eight excited pheasants on the greensward. They were standing in a rough circle chirping. Then I saw the stoat. He was rolling, bouncing and twisting in the middle of the ring. The birds were so fascinated that they drew nearer and nearer with their necks outstretched. Suddenly the wily stoat stopped his antics, and made a rush. He was quick, but the pheasants were quicker. The ones in his line of fire jumped straight up, and let him pass harmlessly underneath. But the stoat was not in the least discouraged. Back he came, and went through the whole performance again. I acted then, but the performer bolted. That bit of trickery showed a fair degree of intelligence, and I have noticed often that the stoat is an astute gentleman. But his intelligence has limits. One incident proved that to me.

A worker on this estate keeps some hens in a pen near the shore of Derwentwater. Wire-netting goes all round the pen, and inside that netting is the hen-house. The nesting-boxes inside the hen-houses have each an earthenware nest-egg. About three summers ago these pot eggs, as they are called locally, began to disappear. The estate worker was mystified. The mesh of the netting was too small to let through a pot egg ; there was no hole whereby a dog could enter, and a squirrel even could not have climbed the netting fence with such a large object in its forepaws. So the perplexed man asked me one day to solve the mystery. I had, therefore, a good look round the pen, but was forced to admit defeat. At length I decided to set a trap. I got a pheasant coop, placed it in the pen near the hen-house door, put a pot egg in one corner, and set a trap in front of it. The spars of the coop kept the hens away from the pot egg, and, incidentally, also from the trap.

Next morning there was a rat in the trap ; so we decided that the mystery was solved, except for the fate of the dummy eggs. The owner of the hens was relieved, but his relief was of short duration. The pot eggs, and probably real ones also, disappeared as regularly as before. I set the trap again, and caught a bitch stoat. She was obviously the culprit, because the pot eggs remained in their nests afterwards. Weeks later all the missing pot eggs were found buried in a mole run under one of the bushes. The stoat had evidently benefited little from experience. She removed good and useless indiscriminately. How long she would have carried on is a matter for speculation, but the owner of the hens retrieved sixteen dummy eggs.

Stoats are like foxes in one respect. They are wasteful of food. Rabbits are killed and left to rot with only the merest bite eaten from the back of their necks. Now and then a stoat will return to its kill for a second helping, and occasionally one will eat the best part of its victim in several feeds, but wastefulness is the general rule. It seems to me that only necessity makes them return to their old kills. If a fresh rabbit happens to be handy when a stoat is hungry, the previous kill is forgotten.

Weasels

Only once that I can remember have I seen a weasel attack a full-grown rabbit with intent to kill. That occurred in Kinnaird deer park, Angus. I shot the weasel; so I am positive that it was a weasel. Since I came to the hut I have never seen a weasel with any other kill than small birds and mice. That is a strange admission for a gamekeeper to make, especially when every now and then someone tells me that he saw a weasel kill a rabbit on a certain date, and that he picked up the rabbit, and that the weasel looked out from a patch of bracken, or a stone wall, then vanished.

I have heard that story with variations often, but I am convinced that the weasel was almost always a stoat. For one thing, these stories have been told me fairly regularly in the last four or five years, and I have not seen more than a couple of weasels in that time. Stoats are growing comparatively scarce in the Lake District now, but weasels are practically extinct. I did see a weasel lying dead on the road to Keswick last summer, but I have not caught one in a trap for years. The weasel which I saw on the road had apparently been killed by a car.

When I came here, there were nearly as many weasels as stoats. A tunnel trap would catch as many of the one as of the other. Why weasels should be so scarce now I do not know. I can only offer the same explanation as I offer for the stoat scarcity, namely, the vast increase in the fox population among those fells. Certainly they have not been reduced by human contrivances.

The weasel is not so intelligent as the stoat. He will let himself be shot at more easily than his wily cousin. In fact, I see something pathetic about him, despite the common idea that he is a bloodthirsty creature. When I see him pop his head out of a hole in the ground, or from a niche in a drystone wall, and present his pale shirt-front towards me, I feel a twinge of pity for him. There is something in his glazed, beady eyes which tells me that he is being slowly driven to his last frontier, and that he knows it. Perhaps someone will tell me that he still flourishes in another part of the British Isles. If so, I shall be glad. It would be a pity if the weasel went the way of the marten.

Once I had an amusing interlude with a weasel along the road there in front of the wood. I was sitting on a rail in the low hedge at the top of my rearing-field, and I was facing the road. It was a sunny afternoon ; so I stopped longer than usual to gather my wind after climbing the steepish field. A weasel, with a small bird in its mouth, came along the hedge bottom from my right. When it got about six feet from me, it hesitated. Then it ran back for a few yards, but I could see that the creature was determined to be past me. It made another attempt, lost courage, and finally made a detour by the middle of the road. I could have shot it easily, but I wanted to see what would happen.

When it got to the hedge bottom again on my left, it tried to enter a small hole with the bird still in its mouth. It pushed and it pushed, but the bird was too big ; so it dropped the bird, and darted into the hole. In a flash it was out again. This time it tried to drag the bird in, but with no more success. I watched the bird, a hedge sparrow, jigging about at the hole mouth for a few seconds, then I tip-toed forward and pulled against the weasel. The little creature hung on grimly until I got its head clear of the hole. Then it saw me, and vanished hurriedly underground. No stoat would ever have acted so artlessly.

Hedgehogs

Often in the gloaming of a summer evening I have seen him ambling across a woodland ride, or hunting a pasture field. He pays little attention to a human being, provided the human being remains statiorary, but at the least hint of danger he stands at the ready. His snout is withdrawn ; that is the vulnerable part. If the danger passes, out comes the snout from beneath its protecting spines, and off he goes

again. If, however, the danger becomes more imminent, he
rolls into a compact ball of spines until the trouble blows
over. Sometimes the trouble does not blow over. I have
known dogs that would attack a hedgehog savagely, despite the formidable armour. Their mouths might be bleed-
ing, and they might be suffering tortures, but they would
not desist until the poor hedgehog's entrails were torn out.

Where game is preserved the hedgehog can be a nuisance.
He will devour pheasant and partridge eggs, or any other
eggs he can get a hold of, for that matter. And a fine mess
he makes. I have never caught him in the act of putting a
bird off her nest to get at the eggs, but I have no doubt that
he is able to do that.

Twice that I remember, hedgehogs were responsible for
serious injuries to hens. Both were in coops. The hens
recovered with difficulty. Their legs and rear-ends were
severely lacerated. The second hedgehog was caught red-
handed in the middle of the night by an old man who acted
as fox-scarer for us. When he heard the hen cackling that
night, he went to the coop and shone his light into it. He
saw the hedgehog ; so he eased up the back of the coop and
let it run out. Then he levelled his gun, and blew the hedgehog's innards out. He made a mess of it. The amusing part
of that story happened the following morning. A keeper
came on duty without seeing the old man, and found the
mangled carcase. It was a puzzler for him, but he finally
put two and two together. A fox had evidently been astir ;
so down went a trap at the remains. He was greatly morti-
fied when he heard the true story, and it was a long time
before he heard the last of it.

I would hardly say that the hedgehog has as good scenting powers as, say, a fox, but one summer evening when
I was standing by the side of the wood near the beck,
a hedgehog came up to me out of the dusk, and started
to lick my boots. Dubbin was the attraction. I was
using it then instead of blacking. The hedgehog had
winded the stuff from a comparatively long way off, and

evidently believed that it had a certain food value.

Often in the rearing-field I have made uncivil remarks about hedgehogs. They used to nose around the coops looking, I suppose, for left-over feed just as the pheasant chicks were settling under their hens, and although they never molested a hen there, they upset the birds so much that they preferred to lie in the grass around the coops. When I arrived to shut up the coops, the birds would rise and fly all over the rearing-field, where they remained the whole night often, unless an owl or a cat got them.

Hedgehogs, like stoats, have decreased in the last few years, but one can hardly blame foxes for that. If foxes made a habit of killing hedgehogs, one would find the spiny integument sometimes lying somewhere in the coverts and fields. Actually I have never found the cleaned-out skin of a hedgehog anywhere, but a few years ago I found the remains of many hedgehogs which had evidently died of some disease. That, I think, accounts for the decrease. One sees the dead bodies of wild animals so seldom that a sequence of them in a short time indicates that something other than natural decay has killed them.

Perhaps the most surprising thing about a hedgehog is its voice. An animal of its size would be expected to have a feeble squeaky voice, if any ; but on the contrary, it can, if caught in a trap, let out the most blood-curdling screams of any small creature I know. When I heard that noise first on a calm summer night, I stood appalled.

Dogs

The Lake District may be described as a land of dogs. There are trailhounds and foxhounds and Lakeland terriers and mongrel terriers and a vast amount of sheep dogs. There are also some game dogs and a heterogeneous collection of other breeds. My work compels me to pay particular attention to the dogs in this locality. I know their characters more or less, and from that I can deduce to a

certain extent the characters of their owners. There is an
Italian proverb which goes thus : 'Chi va coi lupi impara a
urlare.' It means that those who consort with wolves learn
to howl. And I have noticed that the dog of a mean-
spirited man is apt to be treacherous, and that the dog of a
kindly man is apt to be respectful of human beings, if not
absolutely friendly. Of course, there are dogs that take an
antipathy to certain human beings for some psychological
reason. For instance, a dog that has been kicked by someone with a bag on his back may conclude that all men with
bags on their backs are enemies, and act accordingly. It is
not always easy for an owner to eradicate such deep-rooted
impulses, but if an owner neglects to check such a dog on
every possible occasion, it can turn into a dangerous
menace.

Perhaps only about fifty per cent of people who own
dogs know how to keep them in proper control. That fact
is borne on me very forcibly when I see dogs scouring the
countryside daily, hunting rabbits, destroying game and
their nests, and occasionally chasing sheep. The sheep
chasers are, of course, in greater danger than the game
destroyers. The law is somewhat indifferent to the fate of
game, unless something quite serious has happened, but
sheep are fully protected. Luckily, dogs that actually worry
sheep are not common. Sometimes, however, a young foxhound, eager on the scent of a fox, will worry a sheep that
happens to rise in its path. Then, the other hounds, if they
be nearby, will often join in the slaughter. Lambs are the
most frequent victims, but one can hardly be surprised
when a blood-seeking animal like a foxhound falls in dis-
grace. Nevertheless, foxhounds that worry sheep usually
pay the extreme penalty for their misdeeds like other dogs.
When that happens, I feel sorry for the hounds. Useless
mongrels are, however, in a different category. Their
removal is the removal of a nuisance, but really the blame
for their transgressions lies at the doors of their owners.

This week, as I was making my way to Portinscale Post

Office, I met little Della Woods, daughter of one of the estate men. She was returning from school, and she told me that a terrier was worrying a sheep in a field beside the River Derwent. While I was questioning her about the affair, two men came up on bikes from work. They had also seen the dog at its dastardly job, but the sheep, they said, had been able to get to its feet and break away. The terrier did not molest it further. I had my gun with me ; so the brute was perhaps lucky. Too many sheep have been chased and torn in that locality recently.

The destruction of game, however, is much more common than sheep-worrying by hunting dogs. No doubt, the average dog has enough sense to know that sheep are more closely cared for ; so game has to take the weight of the attack. Every few days I see those canine pests careering through the coverts, or hunting the hedgerows. When they find rabbits in snares, they pull them to pieces, and, incidentally, destroy the tackle also. And they scour the countryside day and night. Last week I heard a dog yapping at intervals all through one night. It woke me several times, and I thought that it had got away with a lead on its collar, and had caught itself on some undercover. No such thing. The brute had spent the whole night digging at a rabbit burrow. I saw an excavation like a fox earth next day.

About a couple of years ago a hunting dog troubled me a lot, which was even wiser than its kind. I had been trapping young rabbits in a hedge root half a mile up the valley, and every morning the catch was destroyed. It did not matter a great deal, because the rabbits were very young, and I was merely killing them to save the farmer's crop, but still I was annoyed when I found the mess each morning. At every hole there were big paw marks ; so I estimated that I had to deal with a sheep-dog.

One evening I went to examine my traps at dusk, and was just entering the field where they were from the end nearest to Newlands Beck. I saw a collie standing immobile about a dozen yards from the burrow. It was looking so intently in the direction of the burrow that it did not hear me, and as its rear end was towards me, it did not see that it was in grave danger. For quite a long time I watched it, then it probably winded me; for it grew uneasy, looked round, and bolted. I did not give it a warning, because I recognised it. When I got to the traps, there was the usual destruction. Every little rabbit was torn out. Bits of fur lay around, and there were big paw marks in the loose soil. The cunning creature had been waiting for another catch to destroy, when I saw it. It knew that there were traps in the other holes, and it was too wise to put a foot into them. I suppose that it would have watched those traps most of the night, if I had not frightened it away. Later, an estate man told me that he had seen it standing immobile near the same place one afternoon.

One dog incident riled me greatly. It happened a good many years ago, but I remember it well, because it was evidence of an ungrateful spirit. A farmer had been some-what poorly, and had got into arrears with his work. His hay was lying in the field, and he and his man were not getting on very well with the lifting of it; so I was asked to give a helping hand for a day, or part of a day. I was not an expert at forking hay, but I agreed to do my best. About an hour after I started, the farmer's dog landed into the field with a dead young pheasant in its mouth. That did not please me. I asked the hired man if the dog was in the habit of doing that often. He replied quite casually and cheerfully that it had caught a lot of young pheasants when the hay was being cut. That made me wonder whether my Good Samaritan act was as fully appreciated as it ought to have been.

Another annoying dog incident occurred one Sunday afternoon. It did not give evidence of an ungrateful spirit, but it showed how indifferent some people can be to the harm that their rambling dogs do. A little girl brought a week-old pheasant to the hut door. She said that it has been wandering on the roadway down near the farm. I asked her if she had seen the hen pheasant, or a dog, near the chick, but she said that she had seen neither. I took the chick down to where she had found it, and I stood quietly for a few minutes. Gradually one little chick then another appeared out of the roughness below the oaks, but there were no more than three of them, and the mother hen was not visible. I laid my chick down near the rest and stood back, hoping that the mother would hear their cheeping. No hen pheasant appeared, and the little chicks wandered in all directions, cheeping pitifully. One ran across the road, through the hedge behind the farm, and finally reached the beck edge exhausted. It would have walked into the beck if I had not gone after it. I took it back, but by that time the others had scattered widely ; so I put the chick into some thickish grass and went away. I could do nothing further. A day or two later, some village youths told me that a woman, pushing a pram, had been on the road near the farm with a spaniel. The dog was hunting vigorously among the oaks. That explained the little tragedy. A whole brood of pheasants had been destroyed, because a woman could not restrain her spaniel. There was no doubt about their testimony. They had also seen the little girl who brought me the chick. She had been some distance off, and had not witnessed the scattering of the brood.

At the moment I have not a dog of my own. My last one was a labrador. Her name was Peggy, and she was a knowing creature. Her life until she was nearly nine years old was spent on the Swaledale grouse moors, where she had never seen a pheasant. Nevertheless, she developed a good nose for pheasant scent, and I really think that she finally preferred pheasants to grouse. Many a pheasant has she retrieved down the Bog that seemed to be hopelessly lost. She worked quickly and efficiently. A wounded cock pheasant can travel a long way in a short time, but he had to be a good traveller, indeed, to evade Peggy.

She started to take fits latterly. The first time that I saw her in one I was astonished. I was walking up the side

of the park near the Kennels. The bitch was in front of me
slightly, and unwittingly I touched her right hind leg with
the toe of my boot. I was looking across the park to my
left at the time. Without warning, she turned to her right
once, and fell unconscious on her side. I forget which side
it was, but there she lay kicking and snorting. I knew that I
could do nothing much for her ; so I stood until she came
round. When consciousness returned, she got groggily to
her feet, and looked around her strangely for a while. Then
she leapt on me, overjoyed, when she fully recognised me
again. I could hardly fend her off. No doubt, she was
frightened by the failure of her vital functions. At the time
I could not make up my mind whether the tap above the
hock had anything to do with her condition or not, but
some time after I decided that it had, although she fell into
many a fit without a touch from anything. Some months
later she got in my way again, and she fell in a fit immediately her leg was tapped. Probably there is a nerve near the
surface at that particular place; I do not know, but things
point that way. Despite that, I am convinced that she was
failing then. She grew latterly quite weak mentally. When she
came out of a fit, she was listless, and her brain was obviously
affected. One morning she was missing. Usually I could
depend on her to be at the door when I got up. I never
chained her, because she never strayed outside the fence.
This particular morning I thought that she must have died
somewhere in the tall bracken. I hunted for an hour or two
around the hut, without finding any trace of her, then I
went off. In the afternoon, Mr. Whitson, the poultry
farmer up the valley, stopped his car, and told me that
Peggy was lying on the roadside near his house. He said
that she was dripping wet, and that she seemed to be in a
dazed condition.

I set off immediately on my bike for Stoneycroft. A
hundred yards this side of the house I saw her on the grass
verge of the road. Before I got up to her I shouted, but she
paid no attention. Normally, she would have bounded

forward, and scampered around me. I went up to her, and tried to coax her on a few yards, then I discovered that she could not walk, so I lifted her, and tried to carry her and wheel the bike at the same time. That proved to be impossible. I, therefore, left the bike, and carried her a hundred yards or so, then returned for the bike. It was a slow progression. To complicate matters, it was a hot day. When I got about three-quarters of the way to the hut, a coal lorry overtook me, and I asked the driver to give Peggy a lift as far as was necessary. Poor creature! She was absolutely exhausted. How far she had been I do not know, but obviously she had fallen into the beck that flows out of Smeltmill Ghyll beyond Stoneycroft. For all I know she might have been within an ace of drowning. A few days elapsed before she got over that adventure, but one could see that she was gradually deteriorating. The fits grew more frequent; her eyes grew more and more vacant. She was the property of the estate, and I had been told to put her down, but I put off the evil day as long as I possibly could.

One afternoon she was sitting outside the hut looking into space. I decided to try her skill with a ball of string. At one time she could catch an object that was thrown over her head very skilfully, indeed. She would spring up and catch a high ball just as easily as she caught a near one, and even if I made a few feints, she still would jump at the right instant. So I went to her with the ball of string, and I pretended that I was about to throw it over her head. She grew interested, and she jumped, but her teeth banged against my hand. I tried again with the same result, then I stepped back a pace and sent it over her head. She made no effort to catch it, and I realised that her poor, worn-out brain had merely been telling her that I was giving her something to eat. When she found that there was nothing to eat, she wandered away. I called to her, and she looked interested for a second or two, then wandered off again. It was evident to me that I had to make a decision; so I got the gun, led her over to the edge of the trees, and after some deliberation with myself, I shot her. It was a quick and merciful finish. Lots of people have told me that they could not shoot a dog that has been their companion, but if the distressing job has to be done, I do not see why one should shirk it. I buried Peggy beside a larch tree, and for a long time I was aware that something about the hut was missing.

Ferrets

A good ferret is a useful ally to the gamekeeper; a bad one is a nuisance and a time-waster. A good ferret is a ferret that will hardly go into an empty burrow, that will let itself be caught easily, and that will not stop up for hours, if it cannot dislodge the rabbit or rabbits. A bad ferret will explore empty burrows, will scuttle back into the hole when one tries to catch it, and will spend hours, even days, inside one burrow. Many an hour have I stamped about on a cold day, fuming, while a bad ferret was taking its own time over matters underground.

Of course, ferrets are amenable to training, but it is much easier to spoil a naturally good ferret than to improve a naturally bad one. The impatient handler who grabs his ferrets roughly as soon as they appear at the mouths of the burrow is storing up trouble for himself. Soon the creatures will be so shy that they will bolt like stoats at his approach, and they will lie up for hours rather than face him. The best of ferrets will become useless with that sort of treatment. If, however, they are allowed to wander clear of the burrow, then lifted gently, they will gather confidence, that is, unless they are naturally wild and ferocious. I had one of the latter kind fairly recently. It was originally the property of three poachers, and I trapped it on Swinside Fell. It was a dog ferret, and quite a big one at that, but it was the dud of all duds. I was patient with it. When I put it into a burrow, I stood well back, so that it did not need to fear an attack from me. I let it emerge, without going near it. In fact, I did my best to encourage it, but it had such a wild disposition that when I made the slightest move, it would bolt into the burrow and stop there. If by chance I happened to get between it and the hole, it would arch its back, and hiss. Probably the poachers did not do it any good, but I am convinced that it had an intractable nature.

In the ferret house with the two bitch ferrets it was a tyrant. It monopolised the food, if possible, and one morning I found that one of the bitches had been bitten through the side of the head. She was in a fearful mess. A great clot of blood covered one ear, and she held her head sideways, as if a nerve had been touched. That riled me, because the bitch was worth fifty of the dog's kind. However, I kept the big ferret. I hoped that it might have been an unintentional bite while they were snapping at a piece of rabbit flesh. Some weeks later I found the same bitch ferret with one of her eyes in a bad state. A clot of blood covered it, and I feared that the sight of it was lost. Straightaway I moved the old ferocious brute into a small box by himself. The bitch ferret grew better. The eye looked queer for a long time, but I think that she had the sight of it intact. Then the big dog ferret became so savage that I could hardly put my hands near him. He was always ready to grab, although in fairness to him, I believe that he was grabbing for food. He would snatch food and hide it, if he did not happen to be hungry. Nevertheless, his lunges made one cautious. Finally I put him down. He was utterly beyond all training.

The bitch ferret which he bit twice was probably the best ferret I ever had, or will ever have. She knew exactly whether a burrow was occupied or not as soon as she put her nose to the entrance. If the rabbits were not at home, nothing could induce her to go underground. When she found a rabbit, she either ejected it in about five minutes or killed it. In any case, she never lay up, unless she were blocked in by the rabbit that she had killed. I could get on with the job, if I were ferreting with her. She had also the distinction of being the oldest ferret that I have ever had, or have ever known of. Her age, when she died recently, I calculated at nearly seventeen years. A most remarkable age for a ferret. She grew quite frail latterly. One day last autumn I saw signs that her time was about up. She staggered and almost fell when walking on rough ground at the mouth of a burrow, and once she fell into a ditch that ran alongside a hedgerow where she was working. I was sorry to perceive those indications of decay, but I realised that she was only mortal. Evidently the elasticity had gone out of her muscles, as it will go out of the muscles of humans in time. After that I took her out very seldom, and I made sure that the day was fairly warm when I did use her ; so she lasted longer than I expected. It was the following January that she died. One day I went into her house with food, and I saw her obviously in distress. She could find no rest. One moment she would be lying on the sawdust of the floor ; the next moment she would be burrowing in the hay of her bed. The following day she was lying dead on the floor. So passed a wonderful ferret. She did the work which she was born to efficiently, and she did not ever show discontent by biting the hand that fed her. We humans cannot do much more than that.

I attribute her longevity to the fact that she spent the most of her life in warm, dry surroundings. Her house was not the usual type of draughty, wooden hutch. It was a stone-built structure with a concrete floor, which was kept strewn with clean pine sawdust. In one corner was a pile of hay. So she was always warm. Moreover, her diet was the most natural diet for a carnivorous animal. It was invariably rabbit flesh. Her drink was plain cold water. I am certain that the customary ferret diet, porridge and milk, or bread and milk, is the main cause of early death. The other cause is dampness, and miserable conditions generally. Ferrets are cleanly animals, and if they are compelled to live in filthy hutches, they will sooner or later give up the ghost.

Ferreting is a comparatively humane method of killing rabbits, but it can be a wasteful one, if rabbits refuse to bolt ; and they do take that notion often. Of course, if the ferreter is prepared to dig every time that a rabbit is killed underground, the loss of rabbit flesh is much reduced, but a lot of time is wasted.

Rabbits usually bolt better to the gun than into purse-nets, because in setting nets the ferreter is apt to make a certain amount of noise. Even if he does not seem to be making much noise, there is always a vibration to warn the rabbits that some heavy object is over their burrow, and there is always the human scent. When using the gun, the ferreter can creep up-wind to the burrow and put his ferret into the nearest hole. Even then there must be some vibration, because I have noticed that rabbits usually bolt as far away from the ferreter as possible. That is not an invariable rule, but it happens so often that I am sure that rabbits are seldom deceived as to the whereabouts of their enemy.

Now and then a rabbit will push his head cautiously out of a bolt hole to see what he is dealing with before he makes a dash from the ferret. If the ferreter makes the least move while he is being scrutinized, the rabbit will go underground, and he will usually stop there. However, if the ferreter stays motionless, he will often gather courage either to make a quick getaway, or to amble a few feet from the hole mouth. A quick shot can sometimes get him before he can run back to the burrow, but I do not favour that very much. One is apt to shoot at the exact second of the rabbit's disappearance ; and it is possible that the ferret is just emerging then. I admit that I have taken such a risk without ever shooting a ferret, but I prefer to raise the gun with a slow-motion movement, and shoot the rabbit sitting. When I ferret, sport is a secondary consideration with me. My sole object is to kill rabbits whether they be running or sitting.

I like to do my ferreting on a warm, sunny day if possible.

Rabbits seem to bolt better then, and even if there is a stick-up, one is not chilled to the bone during the wait. It is true that one can keep warm by digging out the ferret, but I would much rather wait. A burrow that is destroyed by digging is a nuisance to trap. In any case, it is easy to block up the ferret in a side tunnel, unless one knows exactly where it is, and can dig down almost on the top of it. I remember an occasion when a ferret was lost for a whole month underground by unintelligent digging. The ferret was mine, but a farmer and some friends of his had the loan of it for the day. They were ferreting in the farmer's intake, that is, in some fenced-in fell-land, one New Year's Day. The ferret lay-up with them ; so they started excavating without any exact knowledge of where the ferret was. Towards evening they had to give up. The ferret was lost. The farmer got me a ferret in place of the one that I had lent him, and we never expected to see the lost ferret again. One morning, exactly a month later, the ferret appeared as the farmer was looking up at the burrow. It was in a dreadfully emaciated state. It must have lived the whole month on the rabbits which it had killed in some tunnel end. A few days later it died, despite every attention. I wonder yet how the poor creature managed to get enough air. Perhaps it was only blocked in by dead rabbits. In that case, of course, a little air would filter past the carcases. A ferret can smother in one night, if it is well and truly blocked in with soil in a short side tunnel. I have seen that proved quite conclusively.

IV. BIRDS

Pheasants   *Sparrowhawks*   *Jays*

Carrions   *Pigeons*

Grouse

WILD pheasants do not flourish easily on this estate. It is surrounded by too much rough fell country where 'the balance of Nature' obtains too crudely. By the way, I do not understand very clearly what is meant by 'the balance of Nature.' Too many factors seem to be involved. If a law were passed forbidding us to kill any animal, bird or insect whatsoever, so that they could work out their own scheme of things, then we humans could anticipate a poor time, because every living creature has been trying hard since the beginning to appropriate most of the goods of Nature for its own self. The reason why Nature has not been unbalanced long ago is that Nature cannot be unbalanced, at least not for any considerable length of time. She will always swing the pendulum true.

In some of those National Trust Woods where shooting is forbidden, and where friend and foe of wild life are expected to live in harmony together, I have often been struck by the lack of happy bird song in springtime. The Raptores and the Carnivora are masters there, and they pay no attention to the Wild Birds Protection Act. So, to produce a stock of pheasants in this unsuitable district we used to hand-rear them. Some people may question the ethics of rearing pheasants by hand for the main purpose of shooting them, but hardly anyone will deny that the pheasant is an ornament to the countryside. I, for one, like to see the cock strutting about the coverts, his lovely plumage aglow in the spring sunlight ; and I like to hear his challenge call echo over the meadows at mating time. And I also like to hear his flutter and chortle as he goes to roost in the thicket on a frosty winter evening.

Eggs for hand-rearing are procured either from a game farm, from one's own pens, or they are collected in the hedgerows and coverts from the wild stock. We used to get our eggs from the first two sources. Any birds that nested in the woods were allowed to hatch their own broods, but we did not count on them to increase the stock of pheasants greatly. Foxes found a lot of those wild nests. They were very often pillaged just as they were about to hatch. Whether a nest has more scent then, or whether the cheeping chicks give the show away, I do not know, but the fact remains that foxes often found them, when one thought that they were doing well.

The game farms send their eggs out usually in wicker baskets, and each egg is carefully wrapped in wood-wool. It must take hours to pack those eggs; I know that it used to take valuable hours to unpack them. Each basket, if I remember rightly, contained five hundred eggs. The price per hundred varies according as to whether it is late or early in the laying season. Early eggs are dearer, but I believe that they are ultimately cheaper. They are more fertile, the birds are stronger and more easily reared, and it is more convenient to have the birds into the coverts early, so that they shall be fully grown by November. Pheasants can legally be shot in October, but big shoots are delayed until late November usually. The birds are mature then, unless they have been very late hatched, and the foliage is off the trees. And in any case, the shooting men are busy with partridges and grouse until November.

Pheasants for the laying pens are caught up in wire-netting traps as soon as the shooting season closes. They are either pinioned with a thong, or they have one wing clipped. If they were allowed the full use of their wings, they would fly out of the pens, which have generally open tops. Even if the tops of the pens were netted, the birds would still have to be clipped or pinioned, otherwise they would injure themselves by flying against the netting when alarmed. Some estates use small movable laying pens ; we favoured permanent pens that covered perhaps half an acre each.

There ought to be some cover in a laying pen, bushes, brushwood, rushes or rough grass ; for pheasants dislike to be in a place where they are unable to hide somehow. Moreover, they need cover in which to lay their eggs. When they start to lay, they try to have some sort of nest, just as if they were at liberty. As the season advances, however, and they find that their nests are being robbed, the eggs may be dropped anywhere in the pen. That cannot be avoided, and carrion crows, magpies and jays often appear for an easy feast. Those birds can take great toll of valuable eggs, if one is not vigilant.

When a few hundreds of eggs have been gathered from the pens, and mixed with a hundred or two of bought ones to keep the strain healthy, the keeper thinks about setting some hens. First of all he scours the countryside for broodies. I used to enjoy that job immensely. One met different people ; for we often travelled a dozen or two miles in a day, if we had a motor wagon. Even when we went with a spring cart to farms near at hand, we always had a pleasant day out.

One had to be pretty alert, though, otherwise there was a chance of being 'done'. I do not mean that anyone would actually try to swindle us, but some people did attempt to foist hens on us that were not broody, if they wanted rid of them for any reason. And there were hens that were dear at any price, even although they were broody. They were so wild and uncertain that they might have destroyed four times their value in eggs, if we had taken them. With all our care we occasionally took a hen that eventually sent the setting of eggs up against the back of the hatching-box. So I always contrived to see a hen actually on its nest before I lifted it, unless I knew the owner very well. If I went to a distant farm, and the poultry woman told us to shut the stable door, or whatever door it might be, in case the hen rocketed out into the yard, my henchman and I got into the wagon and sought fresh scenes.

Some people would have sold all the hens they possessed for ready cash ; others hummed and hawed, and tried to force up the price. But we never altered our figure either up or down. It is not a wise policy to give different prices for the same type of fowl, or for the same type of anything, for that matter. News travels sooner or later, and the person who has accepted less than his or her neighbour nurses a grudge, which eventually operates against the bargainer.

Now and then we were asked into farmhouses for a cup of tea. Usually we declined, because time pressed, but one forenoon we accepted the friendly offer. The real owner of the hens was expected back from Keswick at any moment, and there was the prospect of a good haul of broodies ; so we thought that a wait could be pleasantly filled in by drinking a cup of tea. The housekeeper, or whatever she was, took us into the roomy kitchen, where the remains of a breakfast were still on the table. The unwashed dishes were in their original places, and the milk jug looked as if birds had roosted on it for weeks. Not an appetizing lay-out. But the last straw was reached when our tea was poured into those unwashed cups. A big, middle-aged man with a stubble of whisker on his face, and also unwashed, partook of a friendly cup with us. He kept up an animated conversation, but I am afraid that none of us was interested. When we got outside, the lorry driver, who was not a faddy man, voiced his opinion of the menage in somewhat strong terms. I echoed his sentiments. However, the owner of the poultry arrived, and we got a good few hens ; so our suffering was not entirely in vain.

One day we scoured a considerable part of West Cumberland for only a score or so of hens. I was rather discouraged with our poor bag, but could do nothing to better it ; so we set off home. At Bassenthwaite we stopped at a place, and got no hens there, but were told that a farm eight miles back, which we had missed, had fifty broody hens for disposal. That was too good to miss ; so the wagon driver obligingly turned about, and we were soon at the poultry farm.

A youngish man greeted us. He assured us that he had fifty hens at least that would sit like stones. We could back the wagon into the field, he said. So we backed the wagon, and we took with us a great pile of sacks. Then the young man went into the first fowl-house, and prepared to pull out the hens for us. I said that it would be more convenient if I got the hens off the nests myself, to which he agreed, but I saw that he grew less cheerful. Hen after hen I raised carefully. Almost every one was a layer. When we got to the last house, I had bagged only fifteen hens that were broody. In those pre-war days hens were not so valuable as they are now ; so the chappy had decided that our cash was as good as anybody else's. If I had taken the whole lot without trying them myself, the estate might have lost in re-selling them, and in any case, they would have been a nuisance. I do not say that they would have destroyed many eggs, because we always put newly-brought-in hens on dummies for the first few days, but a laying hen tears the nest to pieces, and that is a vexation and hindrance.

While the collecting of broody hens was going on, we were setting eggs in the nesting boxes every few days. Our nesting boxes were in units of six, had no bottoms, and were set in the open. The hatching of the eggs was, there-fore, as natural as possible, except that the foster-mothers were closed in. The doors hinged downwards in front. Some had no hinges. They were held by two tongues at the bottom and a turn-button at the top, but they were a dis-tinct failure. The hens, when they were being removed, pulled the doors forward among the keeper's feet, and caused delay. Every second counts when several hundred hens have to be taken off their eggs. We contrived to take them off in batches of a hundred and over, which meant that the first one was almost ready to go on again as soon as the last one was removed. Each hen was tethered in front of its own nest by a peg and cord loop. If the loops are lying ready opened, two expert men can take hens off their eggs without breaking any at an amazing speed. The hens were fed once a day on Indian corn and wheat. They also had a supply of grit and water. Now and then a hen would cease to be broody for no apparent reason. Perhaps she would give warning by being always on her feet when the nesting-box door was opened, or she might scrape the nest to pieces and destroy the eggs some day when she got tired of sitting. If she were of the latter order, there were maledictions. If she were of the first order, the eggs were often late in hatching, even under a fresh hen, and the hatch was generally poor. A hen that is preparing to give up very often 'sings'; so we kept an ear cocked for the 'singers.' That saved a lot of trouble.

As the hatching proceeded, the rearing fields were being put ready to receive the pheasant chicks. Coops were placed twenty yards or more apart, on meadows that were as smooth as it was possible to get them. The coops had no bottoms ; so the meadows had to be smooth, otherwise the chicks might have found holes whereby they could have got out when the coops were shut up at night. Chicks have occasionally got out to my knowledge. Some died of starvation, if they were very small ; others were killed by vermin, and the lucky ones were cheeping round the coop when one came to open it in the morning.

The rearing fields had also to be clean ; which means that they had to be free of fouling by poultry, or the fouling of a previous pheasant-rearing. Woe betide the poor keeper who has to rear on foul ground. His troubles are without end. He will find dead birds every day, until he takes his charges to the woods. And his troubles may not end there, but the birds that have survived the foul rearing-field will at least be five or six weeks old. That is some small satisfaction.

The commonest disease in a rearing-field is gapes. It can

kill young birds very quickly itself, but I think that it also
paves the way for other diseases. Should the weather be
good, a slight touch of gapes when the birds are about a
month old may not be at all disastrous, but if the disease
appear earlier, and the weather be cold and wet, then there
is cause for anxiety. The chicks may easily die in hundreds.
I have seen them die in hundreds.

But before our pheasant chicks saw the rearing-fields,
they spent a day or so of their lives in an artificial incubator ; at least, most of them did. When the eggs were
well chipped in the nesting-boxes, we took them to the
incubator for the final stage, excepting for three or four,
which were left with each hen. Her handling of these few
decided her worth as a foster-mother. If the hen trampled
the chicks, or pecked them to death, she was thrown out,
but the loss was small. If, on the other hand, she tended her
little brood carefully, she was allowed to go to the rearing-
field with a full lot of perhaps sixteen chicks. A good hen
can easily cover such a brood. I once tried to dispense with
the artificial incubator for the final hatch, but I will never
do that again. I lost quite a few birds unnecessarily, and I
found out that even the best of hens will trample chicks in
the confined space of a nesting-box, if the brood is too
large.

The boxes which we had for taking the pheasant chicks
to the rearing-fields were fitted with hot-water bottles.
That obviated any chance of a chill to the little creatures,
because sometimes our fields were a mile or more from the
nesting-boxes. They were left in the incubator until they
were thoroughly dry, and able to jump about strongly, but
without the hot-water bottles they might have perished on a
chilly day. One hardly expects a bitterly cold day in May,
but I once had snow lying in a rearing-field.

When the hens are finally settled into their coops, they
may not have any of the chicks that they hatched themselves. But they do not mind that at all. So long as they
have hatched and dried chicks under them they will take a

full brood willingly as a rule. Some hens that are good cluckers may have more than their own brood at the end of the first week. But there are hens that can recognise and resent strange chicks from nearby coops. Such hens will peck the strangers and occasionally kill them. A chick with any peculiarity has to be wary. It is so obviously a stranger when it goes pecking at another coop that it is liable to get a blow from the least observant hen.

While the birds are in the rearing-fields the coops are shut up every night. That is an easy matter for the first week or two, but gradually the little pheasants stop out later and later. Then perhaps some sultry night when they are nearly six weeks old they will decide to stop out altogether. When that happens, they ought to be removed to the coverts as soon as possible. Only once or twice have I been able to keep my birds in the field for the full six weeks. The better the birds the more difficult are they to shut up. It is a nerve-racking job to shut up wary pheasant poults. I usually threw back the doors far behind the coops after the last feed, so that I could approach from the rear with some sort of an advantage, but even so, the alert creatures have rocketed out into the dusk. A chilly evening makes then snuggle into the foster-mother's feathers ; so I always hoped for a chilly night before the birds were shifted to the coverts.

Some keepers shift during the hours of darkness immediately after the shut-up, but we preferred to rise at daybreak, and shift in good light. It is, I think, the better method. All sorts of little disasters can occur in darkness. Pheasants get their legs broken when the sacking is drawn under the coop before it is lifted on to the lorry or spring cart ; or the vehicle lurches over obstructions in the dark woods, and upsets the coops, so that birds get out. Occasionally a coop is set down in a hidden place, and the birds are shut in most of the following day before it is found. In daylight those annoyances are avoided, and the whole operation takes much less time.

When the birds are in the woods, the coops are left open at night. Vermin begin to take their toll then. Many an anxious time I have had when the pheasants were in the woods. I have been driven nearly demented by owls, hawks, cats, foxes and dogs. But one can have anxious times in the rearing-field also, even if the coops are shut up at night. One wet season I had gapes badly in two fields. Birds had been reared in them the previous year, but I was compelled to use them again. Deaths were frequent. In fact, not a day passed without my picking up several dead birds. Things grew so serious that it was decided to shift the coops to some clean ground near the beckside, which is, of course, at the valley bottom. Gradually there was an improvement. The dead birds were still dead, but the remainder grew brighter. They grew interested in life ; and a young pheasant must be interested, or it will pine and die. I was encouraged. I saw that the chicks were getting the insect food which was lacking in the fouled fields. The six weeks were drawing to a close. Soon the birds would be into the coverts, what was left of them. One calm night, about three days from the shift, I shut up the birds with difficulty. They were growing so lusty, and the evening was so serene, that they did not want to go into their stuffy coops. I shut the final coop at midnight, then I made across the dale to bed, dog-tired. I slept like a log, I daresay, because I was conscious of nothing until six o'clock a.m. When I woke, rain was lashing furiously on the roof of the hut. I was not alarmed, but I wished that it had not been raining so hard. When I got out, and saw the valley, I was alarmed then. A full-sized flood was covering the low-lying land near the beck, and scores of the coops were under water. I must add here that the coops had been pegged to the ground on account of wind ; so most of them stood firm until they were submerged. I went down and let the birds out on the parts that were not inundated, but the flood still rose. Many of the coops that I dragged clear of the water I had to drag clear again. In some coops that had only a few inches of water in them the little pheasants were perched on the old hen's back, and when I lifted the coop clear, they had enough sense to fly out of the flood. One or two coops broke their moorings, and sailed away on the spate All the birds in them were drowned, including the hen. These coops finally came to rest against the first hedge, which was by the lane side that leads to the village. Then the flood subsided as quickly as it had risen. About ten a.m. there was only a trickle of water in the fields. The sun came out, but its cheery beams that morning were a mockery. Young pheasants and hens were lying about dead. Coops were upturned everywhere. The coops that had been saved were in a mass near the debris line, but the old hens clucked to their broods when we threw down feed as if all were well. We picked up the dead in sacks. That was a freak storm. Never have I known such a rapid rise of water in the valley, and I have seen a flood or two. There must have been a veritable cloudburst back among the fells. That disaster happened many years ago when there were several keepers here. Two others had their rearing-fields flooded also. They lost as many as I did. That was a warning to us never to have a rearing-field in the bottom of this valley, nor any other valley, for that matter. I have seen water running through pheasant coops on a slope during a thunderstorm, and that can be bad enough for very young birds.

Before we decided to peg down our coops we suffered some minor havoc from winds. I have seen the coops blowing about the rearing-fields like newspaper. Rather surprisingly, not a great many birds were killed, but the disorganisation was colossal. The chicks did not know where to find their own mothers, because the hens when they were caught were put into the nearest empty coop. If the chicks happened to be very small, they had to be caught also and put in with any hen, otherwise they would have starved to death. But they would not stay with any hen, if they had been a few days in the rearing-fields. The result was that when the coops were opened again, the chicks went cheeping all over the place in search of their mothers. Many starved themselves to death in their travels.

Once I saw a field of coops smashed to matchwood. Luckily, there were no birds in them. They had merely been spaced out, and the first hatch was still in the nesting-boxes. One could hardly believe that coops could be so completely disintegrated by wind. They were simply splinters, and some of the splinters had been blown over a six-foot-high stone wall on to the fell. When the estate carter took them to the field, they were piled high on a lorry. When they came back, they were compactly piled on a spring cart.

In addition to the ravages of disease, pheasant chicks die from many causes. Strong, healthy birds will choke themselves on slugs. I have lost a lot from that irritating cause, but I discovered that if I waited until the sun got on to the rearing fields before I let out the chicks that the mortality was lessened ; and I discovered also that the eastern side of the valley was worse for slugs than the other. Cuckoo-spit is another source of trouble on a rearing-field. The chicks swallow the little insect, I think, before it starts to spit, then when the insect gets among the moisture of the crop, it sends out foam. Very soon the bird is suffocated.

Occasionally I have had birds dead in a peculiar snare. They have swallowed the head of some grass, still attached to the stalk, and found that they could not disgorge it again. Thus have they perished miserably, tugging at a mere stalk of grass, which they could not break.

Sometimes a bird gets its head squashed flat between the door of the coop and the sparred front when the keeper is shutting up for the night. The birds that get caught in that manner are usually robust, alert creatures. They hear the keeper's approach better than the others, and prepare to make a dash before the door is slipped on. If they are quick enough, they get out, and the rest follow ; but if they are not just quick enough and the keeper is in too much of a hurry, there is a crunching sound, and another bird may be subtracted from the count. I very rarely killed a bird with the door, because I never slammed it on tight at once. I slipped the bottom into the tongues on the bar, then held the door loosely for a second before I pushed it close up.

Now and then, the keeper will squash a bird with his feet as he goes from coop to coop. That is liable to happen if the keeper is overworked. He has to be getting a move on to finish one feed before another starts. A hundred coops are, I think, too many for one keeper, but I have heard of keepers who attended to a hundred and fifty. Too many coops make a hard, nerve-racking job, especially if vermin are harrying the fields. The coops have to be shifted every day, usually in the forenoon, and if they are pegged down for wind as ours were, the shifting is a long, weary process. When birds are very young, one has to be careful with the shifting of the coops, but with all the care in the world, deaths are bound to occur, if time is limited.

There are many ways of decreasing birds in the rearing-fields, but few ways of increasing them, unless one keeps on setting late eggs. That is, I think, a method that is not worth the bother. The birds are invariably less robust than the earlier ones, and in any case, they have to go to the coverts with the rest, when they are still small. They are then easy victims to vermin, and if the coverts are gapey, they will get the disease almost as soon as they get there.

Some keepers have an ingenious method of increasing their average per coop. They simply take a few of the worst hens away, and divide their birds among the rest of the hens in the rearing-field. If they have, say, a hundred and twelve hens and fourteen hundred pheasant chicks in the field, they may remove twelve hens just before they go to the coverts. They are thus able to say that they reared four-teen birds to the coop, which is pretty good rearing. If they tell that tale often enough, they begin to believe it themselves. It is incredible what people will believe, if they wish to believe.

As the birds grow bigger in the coverts the foster mothers

are removed gradually, perhaps a dozen at a time, until
only the pheasants remain. When that happens, the keeper
can feed the pheasants in one mass as if they were fowls.
He gives a whistle at feeding times, and the birds flock
round him. They are not absolutely tame, however. A
stranger with the keeper may cause them to hold back.
Even if the keeper is wearing anything unusual, the birds
may be suspicious. They are always ready to lift in a mass,
and fly to cover from their feeding place, which is usually
on a ride ; so one has to be careful not to let mass hysteria
take them. When a hundred or two, or more, birds rise
en masse some are apt to fell themselves on tree branches.
A sparrowhawk swooping through the wood can make
them scatter quickly, even although they are too big for
the hawk to kill easily.

Soon after the pheasants become full-grown, or even
before that, they begin to wander comparatively long dis-
tances. They generally return in the late afternoon for their
feed, but some betake themselves to pastures new. No
amount of driving-in with dogs can stop that. There will
always be the restless ones that never return. I proved that
often when we had any birds with peculiarities. Several years
we reared Versicolor pheasants among the ordinary ones.
They are the niggers of the pheasant world, and very handsome birds they are. I shot them, and I daresay other people
shot them, miles from the coverts. It is no exaggeration to say
that when we hand-reared pheasants, we provided shooting
for all the little land-owners around us. Since we stopped
rearing there has been a decrease in the pheasant population
all over the district.

Perhaps some of those permanently-straying pheasants
visit their home coverts now and then in their restlessness,
but only once can I remember one that came back after
years of absence to settle down again among the scenes of
its early days. What made this hen's case so peculiar was the
fact that she had never been seen in the neighbourhood in
the interval. She had a lame leg, and she was tamer than

H

most; so there was no difficulty about her identity. She brought out a brood in this wood a year or two before the war, and as I had fed her often from the door, she used to bring the brood with her.

One evening I was sitting through in the bedroom reading. I heard a tapping on the floor through in the kitchen, but I paid little heed to it. When I finally decided to look, I saw the hen with her whole brood inside the hut. Some of the chicks, birds about a month old, were on the table, pecking away at a few tiny crumbs. I shepherded the visitors outside, and gave them a proper feed there. Often after that I saw them again beside the hut, but as the year advanced they disappeared. Even the old, lame mother bird ceased to be visible in the wood. She went completely, and I thought that she had met her end somehow.

Now comes the surprising part. About two years later the same lame hen came hopping to my door. There was no mistake about her whatever. I threw her some bread, which she ate readily. Most pheasants will not eat bread. At least, they will not eat it when it is thrown to them for the first time. I have tried them often; so I know that. The hen, I say, ate the bread without hesitation, and she went to roost in a fir tree beside the hut. Day after day she appeared again for a feed, and regularly she roosted somewhere near. Sometimes she would come right into the hut, if I did not see her outside. One evening that I remember vividly I was sitting by the fire reading. I was engrossed in my book. The daylight was fading. Suddenly I heard a scraping on the threshold of the open door. I looked round with a pang of contrition as I realised that I had not fed my hen pheasant. She stood there looking at me pathetically with a beady eye, her poor deformed foot trailing on the floor; then she hopped out on to the doorstep in front of me, and I gave her the delayed supper. A few minutes later I heard her flutter up to roost among the firs.

She met her end very swiftly sometime during the following winter. I was sorry, very sorry, but I suppose that she had had a fairly long life. There was no pheasant-rearing that year, nor had there been any for several years, but we used to organise a small shoot now and again. I lined the four guns in the glade here so that they faced up towards the main part of the wood; then, with the help of some estate men, I drove down the steep bank of conifers to them. The backs of the guns were towards the roadside strip. There were only a few birds in the drive. A couple or so were shot dead beside the guns, and another fell in the roadside strip about thirty yards from the front of the hut. The gun who had shot it went into the strip with his dog. I was just behind him. It occurred to me that the lame bird might be hanging about near the hut, despite the shooting, and I wished to tell the gun not to shoot her. I know that he would have obliged me, even although we were out for pheasants. Before I could say anything, a bird rose in front of the dog, went rocketing through a gap in the trees, and was shot dead as it became silhouetted for a second against the evening sky. Thus perished my lame hen pheasant. The gun was very sorry when I told him what had happened, but there was no more tapping on my threshold at dusk. I still have a photograph of her standing just inside the door. Poor, pathetic creature.

The last time that I reared pheasants was in 1939. With the help of a local man, I reared about a thousand. We had two fields on the slope below Swinside Cottages, which is on the opposite side of the dale from the hut, and about half a mile up. It was quite a pleasant summer, but we were harried a lot by sparrowhawks and kestrels. Then, of course, the shadow of war was hanging over the country.

It was in those fields that I became convinced that the kestrel can do as much harm among very young game birds as the sparrowhawk, and show more audacity even. One forenoon when I was giving the birds their second feed, one dropped like a stone from Swinside Crag, and tried to grab a bird between me and the coop that I was just going to feed. I rattled my buckets which made it miss, but it

rose only a few feet and tried again. By that time I was a
dozen yards from it ; so it missed again. Sparrowhawks can
be very brazen, but I have never known one so determined
as that kestrel. There is one good point about the kestrel.
It will not bother birds after they are well-grown.

A farmer's dog killed the whole of a brood for me in those
rearing-fields. It was a rainy evening and coldish. Most of
the birds were under their foster-mothers. I made myself
some supper, and shut the hut door for comfort while I ate
it. About nine o'clock I looked out. I saw a dog in the
middle of the field nearest the feed hut. It seemed to have
something in its mouth, but as the hens were not making
any noise, I thought that it had dug up some dead bird that
I had buried. Nevertheless, I fired a barrel over its head to
scare it away. When I was shutting up an hour or more
later, I noticed that there was little commotion in a coop in
the other field. I took off the door again, and was annoyed
to find that the coop was empty practically, except for the
old hen. Three or four birds from neighbouring coops had
also gone. That part of the field was just out of sight from
the feed hut, and the hens had made no noise ; so the dog
had simply worried the lot without interruption. If I had
known what the dog was up to when I saw it, I might have
made it hurry away even faster than it did. It is a peculiar
fact that the foster-mothers will scream their heads nearly
off when they see dogs or vermin near their broods when
the birds are two or three weeks old, but often they will
ignore dogs or vermin if the birds are very small. They
seem to spend all their energies then in fussing and clucking.

One Sunday afternoon a stranger came across from the
Keswick-Buttermere road to me. He introduced himself,
and said that he had decided to give me a call while he was
in the Lake District. I was somewhat surprised at this, until
he told me that he had read and enjoyed my poems often
in *The Gamekeeper*. He told me that he had even written to
the Editor to find out whether I were a Scotsman, but
Mr. Page had been unable to gratify his curiosity. This

admirer of the Muse came from Fifeshire, if I remember
rightly. I have never seen him again.

At length the young pheasants were taken to the coverts,
but they were not lifted in one lot. Through a fortnight's
delay in the delivery of half the eggs from the game farm
there was too big a difference in the ages of the birds to
permit of their being taken to covert in one lot ; so I had
half of my birds in the woods and half in the fields for two
weeks, which was an extremely inconvenient arrangement.
If there had been two full-time gamekeepers on the estate,
all would have been well ; but my helper had his regular
hours. He conceded a point by stopping until six o'clock,
but from that time until nearly eight o'clock next morning,
they were at the mercy of hawks, owls, cats and foxes. I do
not know how many birds I lost in that fortnight, but I did
lose some.

When the fields were finally cleared, things were much
easier. I took up my abode in the wood with the birds,
which were put down about a mile from this hut near
Derwentwater. Day and night I lived with my charges.
The weather during the summer and autumn was comparatively good, and I rather enjoyed the tinker's life which
I led then. I had no fire in my hut. It was out in the open
air. The hut, by the way, was a lot smaller than this one.
It had only one room. My bed spanned the end farthest from
the door, and my table was a home-made affair of boards by
the doorway. I did have a chair. My bagpipes were under
the bed. When I felt inclined for music, I pulled them out,
and played a pibroch to the roosting pheasants. The feed
hut was nearby. Trees surrounded the encampment entirely, and a steep bank of rhododendrons and hardwoods
sheltered it from the prevailing stormy quarter, which is
Newlands Valley.

Rumours of war persisted, and one Sunday evening a
couple, out for a walk, called to tell me that war had been
declared that morning. I lay on my bed a long time after
those two people went. For an hour or two I thought about

the disaster that had overtaken the world. How it would affect me I did not know, but I expected the worst.

The first pheasant shoot ought to have been in November, but the declaration of war stopped that ; so I continued to feed my birds, and I stopped in the wood with them. Gradually the golden tints of autumn faded. Winter came and still I remained in the wood. My hut began to grow chilly at nights, and the long evenings were monotonous. Once or twice I foiled poachers, who probably thought that I could not stop in the wood in cold weather. Actually I only stopped in the wood to prevent poaching.

Then the snow came, and it came in earnest. I floundered to the knees, if I went far from the hut. The pheasants floundered also. They would fly from the trees at daybreak, and nearly bury themselves when they landed. I cleared the snow from their feeding place ; so they soon knew to fly straight on to it from their roosts. They came swooping through the snow-laden trees as if they were being driven by beaters. But the snow was not the worst discomfort for me. I could stand that. It was the below-zero temperature that got to the marrow of my bones. The temperature was only below zero on two nights, but it hovered so near to it on many other nights that the cold to me was almost uniformly intense.

One brilliant moonlight night I went across to the Big House for something. I remember that the cook was making potted meat, and she gave me a piece to take back to the hut. It was gloriously beautiful in the snowy woods, but I shivered as I stumbled through the drifts. The air had a razor edge. I put the potted meat on the table, and got into bed before my feet froze. I had no means of warming myself other than by exercise ; so it behoved me not to let myself get chilled. I slept well I remember. When I awoke, I might have imagined that I had been transported to the Arctic. The rude walls of the hut were covered with ice crystals, and on the bed counterpane was a patch of white ice where my breath had been freezing.

When I got up, I found that my boots were frozen hard to the floor. The cold was enough to make one desperate. I lighted the fire outside with difficulty, and piled on as much wood as I could possibly get between the circle of stones. I decided to have a piece of potted meat for breakfast. It was like eating grit. The watery cells in the meat had frozen hard. My tea went cold in a few seconds. However, I had plenty of food; so I ailed nothing as far as the inner man was concerned. Then I had a wash and a shave. My breath froze on the mirror, so that I saw nothing in it. It was tough going. The birds clustered on their feeding place. They did not mind the cold much. They sparred and argued with each other as usual. I gave them a good tuck-in of Indian corn and wheat, then I piled all the wood I had in hand on the fire, and tried to get some heat into myself. After dinner my wood was gone. The feeble winter sun started to leave my camp, and I felt that if I stopped there in that temperature something would happen to me. So I fed my birds about two o'clock with a big feed, and I locked the hut door, then I floundered across to this hut for one night at least of comfort. I did not cross the beck bridge down there; I walked over the Holm, and crossed the beck on hard ice. When I got to my own home hut, I made an enormous fire. There was plenty of coal, but I had no water. However, that difficulty was soon solved. I packed the kettle full of snow, and in about half an hour I had a good feed ready. Luckily, my cupboard was well stocked. The war was on, but rationing had not yet come in earnest. When I had fed, I aired some blankets, and I spent the night in comparative luxury. The fire I kept on all night. Next morning I was back at my encampment refreshed.

The game season was getting on, and a shoot of sorts had been arranged, but the snow had caused it to be postponed. Sport was a secondary consideration. The birds had to be shot; that was the main point. Quite suddenly I was told that a few guns were coming out one afternoon, snow or no snow, to have one drive. Some estate men were to act as beaters, and I was told to take my gun. I do not like to shoot my own pheasants, but I took my gun, and joined the shooting men. The drive was simple. We ran the pheasants up into the bank of rhododendrons, then drove them out at a place where the bank was somewhat steeper, which was only about fifty yards from the feed hut. The birds flew remarkably well. It was January ; so they were fully mature and alert. I might as well say here that hand-reared pheasants are not easier to shoot than wild ones. Lots of people who have never fired a shot have told me that anybody could shoot a tame pheasant, as they call it. That is by no means so. A pheasant rocketing over high trees in January can tax the skill of the best shot. A really wild bird may show more ingenuity in defeating the beaters perhaps, but when he does fly in the right direction, he is not more difficult to bring down. And even hand-reared pheasants can become as cunning as their wild brethren, if they are harried often enough. They learn to fly anywhere except over the line of guns.

Thus ended the last shoot of hand-reared birds here. We shot less than a hundred, because they came out of the rhododendrons in big bursts, and we only had the one drive.

Next day I was told to catch the rest up in wire traps. My henchman, Paddy Gilpin, and I, therefore, constructed a long wire-netting tunnel near the feeding place. For a start it had neither roof nor ends, and I fed the birds through it until they became accustomed to the netting. Gradually the birds forgot about the shooting day. They turned up in considerable numbers. I saw that the time was nearly ripe for a haul ; so we put a roof of netting on the tunnel, and we hoped that nothing would scare the birds before we were ready to catch them. A low-flying sparrowhark could easily have alarmed them. Then they would have found out that they were in an enclosure. That would have been disastrous. However, nothing did alarm them, and one morning when the tunnel was full, Paddy and I shut up each end at the same time with bits of netting that we had ready. It was a good sweep. We carried them down to the game larder on a long larch pole, which sagged in the middle. We had other less successful hauls, and finally we had to set a number of little, self-acting traps of wire-netting throughout the wood. In a week or so we had accounted for about seven hundred. The rest defeated us, as the season closed.

It was a poor wind-up, but people then were thinking of more serious matters. So I went back to my fellside hut. Paddy gave me a hand to shift my gear one Saturday mid-day. We only took essentials. I had plenty of tackle in this hut to carry-on with. It was a lovely quiet day in February. I had lived the life of a nomad in the pheasant covert for at least seven months. But no one compelled me to do that, except poachers. If I had gone back to my own abode each night, the pheasants would have gradually vanished.

So Paddy and I staggered on with the household goods. He had a sack of bedding, I remember ; and I had a sack of miscellaneous effects. Underneath my left arm was a set of bagpipes, half-mounted with nickel silver and ivory.

Sparrowhawks

Up in the wood there are several splashes of feathers. Each is mute testimony of a tragedy. There are blackbird feathers, thrush feathers and chaffinch feathers. A sparrow-hawk has glided along those narrow rides, and swooped on the luckless birds almost before they were aware of her presence. And I say 'her,' because all those murders were probably the work of one hen sparrowhawk. I have seen her skim over the sward in front of the hut, and disappear up there among the conifers. Some day she may skim into a charge of No. 5 shot, and the little innocent song-birds will breathe a sigh of relief, if song-birds are able to sigh.

Sparrowhawks have been often a pest to me. My pheas-ants were never safe from their attentions until they were more than half-grown. In fact, I have had hen pheasants killed so late in the year that they could almost be classed as full-grown birds. The killer of those big pheasants was always a hen sparrowhawk. Once I was nearly driven demented by the depredations of such a killer. All over the wood I found kills, a fresh one every day. To set a trap at any of them was useless. That hen sparrowhawk never returned to a day-old feast. She preferred something fresh, and I daresay she found no difficulty in getting it, as there were about a thousand pheasants in the wood then. Seldom did I see the hawk, but the chaffinches and the robins, and occasionally one of the few broody hens that remained, apprised me often that my enemy was astir.

One hot afternoon after I had found a fine bird lying dead I decided to comb the wood carefully, hoping that she might be drowsing in the heat somewhere. I stalked about cautiously with the gun at the ready along the rides first, then I got among the larches and looked each section in turn. After an hour's searching, I heard a rustle above me. That was up near the fell wall. In a flash I had the gun up. The hen sparrowhawk, a big one, was straight above my head as I aligned the gun. It was a quick difficult shot, but she went dead into the larch top in front of her, then dropped to the ground. That was a tremendous relief to me.

Although I quote that case, because the hawk killed birds so late in the year, yet every pheasant-rearing season I was harried to a greater or less extent by those rapacious brutes. Sometimes I kept free of them in the rearing-field, but there was always trouble when the pheasants got to the woods. Hawks came in from far and near. They must have some sort of bush-telegraphy, because no sooner was one removed than another took its place.

One gets an instinct for finding sparrowhawk nests. They are never in dense thickets. Always there is an avenue of some sort leading up to them. Sparrowhawks, apparently, like to have a clear getaway. That habit simplifies a gamekeeper's work when he is searching a wood for their nests.

The sparrowhawk is not usually so cunning as the carrion at her nest. If she be sitting hard, she will return in less than half an hour, as a rule ; but if she has been put off a few times, and has had a shot or two fired at her, she may develop a considerable wariness. I always make a hide when I find a nest, because that practically guarantees a kill, but I have known sparrowhawks that would return to their nests while a person was sitting quietly in a barely-concealed place nearby.

Several years ago I found a nest in a Scots fir tree at the top of this wood. It was a sunny morning. I got myself hidden and waited her return, which was not long delayed. She settled on a larch branch, and I knocked her off. She had been sitting hard. That was evident by the bare patch on her breast. I did not bother to wait for the cock, as that is often a long and sometimes unsuccessful procedure. If there had been young in the nest, I might have got the cock fairly soon. In any case, I congratulated myself on having prevented a rapacious family from growing up to harry the woodland and its environs. A couple of days later, however, I was surprised to get another hen at the same nest. She was also a sitting bird. There was a bare patch on her breast. The cock had found a spare hen somewhere, and he had found her quickly.

The following year I found another sparrowhawk's nest farther along the wood. It was completely built, but no bird was sitting on it. I could not tell how many eggs were in it, as the tree was a slender larch without branches near the ground ; so I decided to wait until the hen started to incubate before I tried to get her. However, that plan went agley, or so I thought. One morning, as I was going along the ride near the nest, a sparrowhawk skimmed over my head. I knocked it down, and found that I had shot a hen. That seemed to me to be the end of the nest ; so I did not trouble further with it. But one day a week or so later I gave the tree a kick as I was passing. A sparrowhawk flew off, obviously a hen sitting on eggs. I made a hide, and shot her.

For some time after that I was busy in the rearing-fields over the dale near Swinside Cottages. There was a steep bank at the bottom of those fields, and the coops nearest that bank started to attract the unwelcome attentions of a hen sparrowhawk. She glided along under cover of the bank, and swooped up suddenly among the young pheasants, usually just after they had been let out in the morning. My helper, a village man, and I tried unsuccessfully to get her; she was too swift and too artful. Then I conceived the idea that she was coming from this wood; so one morning after I had given the pheasants their ten o'clock feed I made across the dale to investigate. I thought that there might be a second nest, which I had overlooked, but out of curiosity, I went first to the nest that I already knew of. When I kicked the tree, a sparrowhawk flew off; so I re-made the hide, waited about half an hour, and I got another broody hen sparrowhawk. That made two off the same nest, almost certainly off the same clutch of eggs, and one near the nest, almost certainly the builder of it. At the time, that seemed very remarkable to me, but since then I have read of keepers who have had similar experiences. Nevertheless, it proves that the cock must go a considerable distance to find another hen to hatch the eggs, because the number of spare broody hen sparrowhawks in any area must be extremely limited. It also proves that the cock has as strong a desire to get a brood reared as the hen. The amazing part is that the cock can find a spare hen before the eggs are useless. On the other hand, I daresay that many a time the cock cannot find a suitable partner in time, and the eggs do go useless, but the fact that he has the instinct to try is astonishing. I can admire those rapacious birds for their devotion to each other, although I have often uttered maledictions against them.

Sparrowhawks can usually be trapped quite easily to their own kills, but practically never to the kill of any other bird or animal. Only once that I can remember have I trapped a sparrowhawk to a bait that I myself laid down.

The bait in that case was a rabbit, and I cannot explain even now why the hawk was attracted by it, unless it was desperately hungry.

When a sparrowhawk returns to its own kill, it very often settles plumb on the top of it. It does not stand back a few yards to survey its meal, then walk in towards it, as a carrion crow does. For that reason, a trap, if it is to do any good, ought to be set close up to the kill, and a twig arranged, so that the hawk must settle on the trap first. Many a time have I seen a sparrowhawk fly away from a kill, which had a trap set close up to it, but which had no twig to foil the hawk. One would think that if the hawk did settle directly on to, say, the remains of a pigeon, that it must step sometime on to the ground at the side of its prey while it was tearing the flesh to pieces ; but that is not always so. The sparrowhawk can devour the lot without leaving its perch on the carcase, then fly away, quite unaware that a trap was concealed three inches from its talons.

Sparrowhawks do not worry me now as they once did. I still give them a barrel, if a chance presents itself, but there is little game to protect. Now and then I see a young rabbit dangling in a set of cruelly sharp claws ; but rabbits do not matter greatly, or so they say. Anyway, my nerves benefit. I do not shudder inwardly now when I hear the screech of frightened song-birds, or the mournful whine of robins in an otherwise silent wood.

Jays

The jay has, with truth, been called the comedian of the woods. I have been deceived often by his mimicry. He can imitate any other bird's voice with complete accuracy. Sometimes his voice lacks the power of the bird's that he imitates, but even so, it is not always easy to tell that the comedian is having a joke. I have heard him imitate an owl, a buzzard, a blackbird, a pigeon and even a carrion crow with fidelity. Often I have been stalking what I thought was a carrion crow, when a derisive screech has apprised me that I have been 'done'. He is great fun, but he is also a great robber of song-birds' nests. And although I have never caught him in the act, I believe that he will devour tender nestlings.

Jays are numerous in the Lake District, too numerous. A gentleman, who lives on the New Road, Portinscale, came to me one day last summer as I was passing his house. He asked me if I could do anything to stop the havoc which jays were making among the birds' nests in and around his garden. Every nest that he knew of had been pillaged. The jays came mainly from the direction of Ullock Moss, he said ; and he had watched them hunt the hedges and bushes assiduously. The parent birds of the despoiled nests made a fearful commotion, but that availed nothing. The robbers carried on with their foul work.

I could have told him all that, and more, because I have experienced it often. Up in the wood here in springtime, one can hear the angry cries of thrushes and blackbirds as they try to chase away their impudent enemy. I sometimes go after the knave, but he is artful then. He does not make the woodland echo with his jeering screech in the springtime so much as he does at other times of the year. Oh, no ; he flits about very silently then. Well does he know that a racket might lead an inquiring human being to where his family is being reared.

The nest is difficult to locate. It is a solid affair that would withstand any amount of shots from a twelve-bore. As the young grow bigger in the nest, the parent birds become tamer usually. They have such an exacting job to fill perhaps half a dozen ravenous maws that they will allow a human being to approach them much nearer than ordinarily. Both birds feed the young, but they appear to have a full-time task. I have watched a pair from my window, and they never halted for a breather. One was always visible, hunting eagerly for grubs and insects.

The comedian is a bold chap, but he occasionally meets

his match in the sparrowhawk. I have seen his beautiful blue wing feathers scattered in the woodland rides, along with the feathers of birds that he has despoiled. And I felt sorry somehow.

Carrions

No gamekeeper will say a good word for the carrion crow. For destructiveness among young bird life and eggs, and even lambs and fallen sheep, it has few equals. Added to that destructiveness is an unbelievable cunning. It is not easy to get the better of Corvus. The hen will refuse to return to her nest for hours, if she suspects that someone is waiting for her. And a hide has to be well made, if it would screen anyone from her keen eyes. But even if she is kept off her eggs for hours, it will be remarkable if the eggs are thereby addled. I do not know how long a carrion crow has to be kept from her eggs before they are addled, but it must be a comparatively long time, because I have never been able to destroy a nest without either shooting the crow, or sending a few shots through the nest. I have waited for hours and hours at a nest, until I almost convinced myself that the eggs must be useless, then the carrion has defeated me in the end by coming back in the dark. One such case that I remember particularly occurred up the valley a few years ago.

It was a balmy spring evening when I found that nest high on the fellside among some scrubby oaks above the farm of Keskadale. When I got my hide completed, the time was about eight o'clock. I was not very well hidden, as the oak branches of the hide were rather sparsely covered with foliage, but I hoped that the carrion would miss me in the diffused light. Vain hope ! The brute glided silently under the trees for a look around first. She had no intention of going to the nest until she had satisfied herself that all was well. So she saw me. At once she darted up through the trees, and was gone, croaking horribly as she crossed the valley. I knew then that I was up against it, as the saying is. I added some more branches to my hide, and sat down for a long wait. Hours passed. I was tormented by midges, but I made as little movement as possible. The day began to fade, and I was a few miles from the hut, but I expected every minute to hear the rustle of the carrion's wings as she settled on or near the nest, so I remained at my post. Gradually the nest began to disappear in the gloom. I trained my gun on to it, so that I could shoot even when I could not see it at all. I was determined to blow it up, if I did not get the hen, because it was too far for a second visit. Then in the velvety darkness I heard a rustle in the direction of the nest. I waited a moment or two, in order that the bird might get on to her eggs. Bang! The silence of the valley was shattered by the explosion of my gun. There was an outburst of angry croaking, which mingled with the racketing echoes of the shot among the fells, and I knew that I was defeated. The cunning creature had not been on the nest when I fired. I was certain of that, as I had marked it well before the light faded. I made my way with difficulty down the stony fellside, and reached the hut in time to greet another day. What the farm people at Keskadale thought about that midnight shot I never knew, but they must have been surprised.

Two years ago there was a carrion's nest at the top of this wood, which gave me some trouble. It was in the top of a Scots fir, and the fir was in turn in the middle of a bed of laurel bushes. That was a complication. I could not get near the tree without making a considerable noise, and if I stood at the edge of the laurels, I could not get a shot at the bird as it left the nest. It always flew out from the side opposite, and kept the whole of the tree top between itself and me. In fact, it was such a cunning brute that I did not always see it leave the nest. I did not want to destroy the nest before I got the hen carrion, but time passed, and I did not see that happy event getting nearer.

One Saturday afternoon I came back from Keswick,

IX. Grouse: Dick Scott's golden labrador retrieving

X. Cartridge cart on the way to the grouse butts

XI. Carrions: Their death means peace for the shepherds
and the song birds

XII. Pheasants: Well grown young birds waiting for their
evening feed

where I had been collecting my meat ration and a few other odds and ends to keep the wolf from the door. A strong gale was blowing. As I approached the hut, I had an idea. The noise that the wind was making among the trees would allow me to get near the nest, if I used some caution ; so I got the gun, and climbed up the wood. At the lower side of the laurel bed I got down on my hands and knees, and crawled cautiously under the bushes, until I was beneath the nest. A flying shot was impossible, but I was not daunted. I aimed the gun and sent a shot into the right place. The carrion was able to flutter off, but that was the end of her. I have never had a carrion's nest in a more awkward position, but I have often had them in high trees and in solitary trees, and these positions are also often difficult.

One evening a farmer's son came to me when I was rearing pheasants up the valley with news of a carrion's nest in a tall oak tree by the beckside immediately below Rowling End Farm. He was an active youth, but he said that the tree was too tall, and the position of the nest too difficult for him ; so I went with him to see what I could do. I took my gun and some B.B. cartridges, which have great penetrating power, much greater, anyway, than ordinary No. 5 or 6 shot.

I had no time to wait for the hen carrion, nor was there the slightest cover nearby, if I had wished to wait ; so I loaded the gun with B.B. and sent a charge into the nest. There was an immediate squawking of young birds. I fired three more in rapid succession, and the squawking stopped. Obviously, I had destroyed the brood. The lad and I talked for a few minutes before I set off again to my fields of pheasants, then he suddenly decided to climb the tree to have a look at the nest. It was a difficult and dangerous feat, but he managed to reach his objective. And it was perhaps fortunate that he did so. Only one young carrion was dead. The other three were alive and quite unhurt. That showed me that even B.B. shot is not always powerful enough to

I

penetrate a mass of sticks in the top of a tall oak tree. Nowadays I never leave a nest in an inaccessible place until the fledgling carrions have dropped out dead, or the whole structure is blown apart.

Anyone who has watched a carrion crow approach a bait of which he is suspicious, can tell how diabolically careful he is to avoid possible traps. He will walk round and round a score of times, eyeing the bait from every angle, then he will pretend to approach it, and immediately fly away. He apparently expects the bait to show its hand in some way or another, and he will keep an eye on it from a distance of a hundred yards. After he has satisfied himself that the piece of rabbit or whatever it may be has got nothing up its sleeve, he will fly back, and alight perhaps a dozen yards from the bait. He will then walk around it another score of times, until he has gathered a little confidence. Step by step he approaches the toothsome morsel. There is no hurry. His beady eyes are fixed on the objective, and he is ready for any eventuality. At last he is about a foot from the bait. Slowly he edges forward, a fraction of a step at a time, leaning back on his elbow joints. He still stares fixedly at the tit-bit, and his beak is aimed at the part that seems most alluring. For half a minute he may stand thus. If caution gets the better of him, he will relax, and go through his circular promenade again ; but if he means business, he will suddenly launch himself on the bait, try to grab the bit that pleases him best, and at the same time brake himself in the act with outstretched wings. If the tit-bit happens to be a rabbit's entrails, and he grabs an end, but finds that the rest is fastened, he will drop the lot, and he will drop it almost as soon as he lifts it. There is no hesitation. I have seen all those antics often. Every carrion does not go through the whole gamut, but practically every carrion does some careful reconnaissance work before it approaches a bait ; so I am never surprised when I find a trap sprung empty, which has been set for a carrion.

During the deep snow of this last winter I shot a lot of

those cunning creatures at various baits from my bedroom window. The great draw, however, was a half-eaten sheep. I found it one afternoon in the roadside strip behind the hut. Foxes and dogs had left only the fore part, but it was enough. The head was intact. I dragged it from the strip over the snow to a position fifty yards from the window, but to the left. If I had placed it directly in front of the window, the carrions might have seen me open the door which connects the kitchen and the bedroom. An incredible amount of carrions were attracted to that half-eaten sheep. I was able to watch their manoeuvres closely. Some were more suspicious than others, but not one flew into the glade and landed straightaway on the bait. Some would have nothing to do with it, although they must have been hungry. There was a yard of snow on the ground.

I did not get every bird that I fired at. It was not that I missed the lucky ones. I could tell from the rake of the shot on the snow that I ought to have killed, but fifty yards is a longish shot, and if I had dragged the sheep any nearer to the hut, the carrions would not have settled within shooting range.

One fact which I noticed particularly when firing No. 5 shot at a range of fifty yards was that the charge dropped considerably. The pellet pattern in the snow showed me that. When I held about six inches above a carrion's head, I did better, but I might have done better still if the carrions had been fifteen yards nearer.

When the snow went, I had forty-two carrions lying behind the hut, and I daresay that a lot died which I never picked. A few of those forty-two I got over the dale in the larch plantation while they were coming to roost, but only a few. Thirty-five at least died in this glade.

One spring evening several years ago I went up to Low Snab, a farm at the top end of the dale, to attend to a carrion crow's nest, which was in a big sycamore tree up the little offshoot valley beyond the farm. The hired lad and the farmer's schoolboy son went with me to point out the nest. The hen bird went off at our approach ; so I started to build a hide. While that was going on, the son, who had been watching interestedly, said : 'Thoo'll nut need ta mak' a varra thick hide ; a carn craw's gitten nobbut a laal eye.'[1] I smiled. The hired lad looked sideways with a disapproving expression at his mate for a second or two, and replied dryly : 'Ay, it's gitten a gay laal eye, but it is a dinged sharp 'un.' And it is a dinged sharp 'un.[2]

Pigeons

Although the pigeon is a toothsome morsel when baked in a pie, I should be inclined to name him as more of a true pest than the rabbit. For one thing he is a cunning bird ; and for another, he may cover miles in the course of his depredations, and is, therefore, difficult to circumvent. One can expect to find the same rabbits in the same circumscribed locality, even in the same burrows, if they are left alone, but pigeons may be here today and gone tomorrow. The fact that the damage they do is not always noticeable does nothing to lessen its significance. Anyone who has shot pigeons has seen the vast amount of grain that can be held in their crops ; and if the crop contents be of a crisp nature, such as cabbage leaves, two hands cupped together would hardly hold them.

The county agricultural committees wage perpetual warfare against those blue marauders. Pests officers organise shoots, so that each wood in a locality is covered by guns on the same evenings, but pigeons flourish, despite that. I seldom lose an opportunity myself of knocking them down, although during the war years, and since then, cartridges have not been easy to get, which compels me to shoot my pigeons, as far as is possible, sitting on the branches of trees.

---

[1] 'You'll not need to make a very thick hide ; a carrion crow's got only a small eye'.

[2] 'Yes, it has got a very small eye, but it's a dashed sharp one'.

(Cumbrian dialect).

I do, however, fire if the flying shot is definitely within range and the obstructions are few.

I have located several places on my ground where I can get a pigeon easily when I have to produce one at short notice. One place is at the top of this wood. The pigeons have a favourite oak, where they can digest their ill-gotten food and survey the valley at the same time. I have a path cut through the conifers and the rhododendron bushes at the top which allows me to approach the pigeons without ever being visible to them. My procedure is simple. Any time I leave the hut I pause for a moment or two and scan the trees at the top of the wood ; then if a pigeon be sitting there, I climb up and shoot him without any trouble at all, except that I must always walk very quietly. Now and then the shot bird is able to flutter into the rhododendron bed below the oaks, but I generally manage to retrieve it. Occasionally one flies away and drops dead before it can get clear of the wood, and the few that I cannot retrieve are retrieved by a fox. The feathers testify to reynard's ability in that direction.

Another place where I can usually get a few pigeons, but never a big bag, is at Ullock Moss, a boggy wood near Portinscale. On a drier part of it is a biggish clump of Scots fir and spruce ; and outside those, but farther into the Moss, are some hardwoods. It is on the hardwoods that the pigeons like to settle before they fly into the warmer conifers to roost. Underneath the hardwoods is a holly bush. It has a thick top, and I have made the middle of it by careful pruning into an ideal pigeon-shooting hide. One can stand beneath the thick foliage without being at all visible to the pigeons on the oak and ash branches above. I never attempt to shoot at the pigeons there in flight. It is not necessary, as the favourite settling place is almost straight above my holly hide.

There is another good pigeon-shooting place in the wood beside Derwentwater. It is a bank of oak, ash and beech trees with tallish rhododendron bushes underneath.

Among such open, but thick-topped undercover it is comparatively easy to stalk pigeons that have settled in the branches of the hardwoods.

During a snowy period some years ago I made my best bag there. Every other source of pigeon food must have been covered with snow, because the pigeons came in scores to that bank to search for acorns and beech mast below the rhododendrons, which had kept the snow from lying deeply on the ground. For several days I did little more than stand under those bushes and fire at the pigeons as they settled in the hardwoods before they fluttered down to their feed. The continuous shooting did not frighten them much. They came back in droves a few minutes after a shot had gone off, as avid as ever. The bushes were heavy with snow as well as the tree branches, and often when I fired through a narrow opening in the canopy, a great cloud of snow would descend on me. Sometimes I could not see the bird fall, so much was I engulfed in the miniature avalanche.

A friend of mine has had good sport on St. Herbert's Isle in the middle of Derwentwater on many occasions. He has counted his kill by the sack. He told me that he glutted the local market once. It was near Christmas, a pre-war Christmas, of course, and every gamedealer was provided with plenty of other fare. Finally he tried to give the pigeons away, but nobody wanted them, even for nothing.

Pigeons come readily to a decoy. When they are raiding newly-sown or newly-harvested fields, they are often lured to within shooting distance of a hide by that method. Considerable bags are made thereby, if pigeons are numerous, but it is a method that I have not practised much. Patience is often necessary, especially if there are several harvested fields in the same area. On the other hand, if pigeons are really coming in numbers, the fun is fast, indeed.

The best (or worst) wood for pigeons on my ground was cut down during the war. That was Swinside Moss, a dense cover of spruce and larch. Lots of pigeons hatched their broods there, and it was a favourite roosting place all the year round. But it was never easy to shoot the pigeons as they came in. They circled the Moss once or twice usually, then descended from a great height, and went flop right into the dark tree-tops, where one could only see them with difficulty, if at all.

When Swinside Moss was being felled, many fledgling pigeons were thrown from their nests. They had to remain on the ground, of course, but the parent birds, usually so wary and timid, continued to feed them while the wood-men hewed away at the timber nearby. That was rather surprising.

One fact which I noted when the Moss was standing was that the pigeons there had two definite breeding times. Lots of young pigeons were to be seen in the spring and autumn, but very few in the summer. Hawks and owls used to take heavy toll often of those immature birds.

The local pigeon population is usually augmented in the autumn by migratory birds. Those immigrant pigeons often come in vast hordes. They may stop for months, or only for weeks. Occasionally they appear for only a few days. Every gunner in the district is out to bag as many as possible while the foreigners are here, but little impression is apparent in their numbers.

Grouse

For eight consecutive grouse seasons, excepting the season of 1939, and beginning with the season of 1936, I went over to our moors in Swaledale to help with the grouse shooting. I went mainly to load for my employer, but between shootings I performed most of the duties of a moorland keeper. One job, however, I did not tackle. That was the setting of those pre-historic stone traps for stoats, which are common along the limestone walls of the North Riding moorlands. The keepers in Swaledale set them in hundreds. They are cheap, certainly, but one has to be

born to the setting of them, I think. The trap is composed of
two heavy, flat stones, one of which is propped up by an
ingenious arrangement of sticks. Those sticks form the
figure 4, and the trap is, I believe, called the figure 4 in some
parts of the country. In Swaledale it is called the 'Samson.'
The idea behind this structure is that, when the horizontal
stick is disturbed by the stoat as it pulls at the bait, the
upper stone falls and squashes the stoat flat. The one great
merit of the trap is that it is humane.

In pre-war days the grouse season was an important
social event. Nobody of any note was seen in town about
the twelfth of August. I was not of much note, but still I had
to pack my suitcase and join the fashionable crowd. I
travelled over in the shooting brake from here, and I got
on to the moors usually a week or so before the glorious
Twelfth. At first I lived in lodgings with a keeper, but in the
last few seasons I lived at the Lodge. My room there was
above the gun-room. It was attached to the Lodge, but my
door led to the open air, so that I could go in and out as I
liked without passing through the main building. I liked
that arrangement. I was almost as free there as I was in my
Lakeland hut. Sometimes the shooting men left their dogs
in the gun-room for the night, and they often fought and
barked, but I could bear that; or if they became too much
of a nuisance, I would go down to them and stop their antics.

The first time I looked on Swaledale I thought that it was
the bleakest place in Britain. The bare landscape, the miles
of stone wall on the pastures at the edge of the moor, and
the grey stone houses repelled me. But I got used to all
that after a season or two. Gradually I got to know the
inhabitants also, and finally Swaledale became a familiar
homely place to me. I had tea often in many of the houses.
Once or twice I took the pipes with me; so my recollections
now of the dale are very pleasant.

Normally the Lodge was only occupied by a caretaker
and his wife, but before the guests arrived a fairly big staff
took possession of the place. The caretaker, by the way, was

also the gardener; his wife acted as cook during the season, and a very good cook she was. The temporary staff was recruited mainly in London, and the individuals of it were a varied lot. They only came for one season as a rule, but now and then one would turn up for several successive seasons. None of the girls that I remember could put forth any great claim to beauty. On the whole, however, they were a pleasant crowd, and one was quite decidedly superior in character to the usual servant.

In addition to the staff, there was always a movable population at the Lodge of shooters, loaders and chauffeurs. A fresh team appeared every week as a general rule; so there was no lack of company, or of fresh faces for the student of human nature. Those men servants were not, I found, very outstanding in anything, excepting occasion-ally in false self-esteem. A peer's chauffeur would some-times imagine that he also wore a coronet. One could easily see that a gamekeeper was small beer, indeed, in the esti-mation of that type. If he deigned to chat to anyone in the gun-room, it would be only to one of his own tribe. But the Lodge was a cheery and interesting place between early August and the middle of September in those pre-war days, despite the occasional little snob. I found the stir there a pleasant change from my somewhat austere life in Lakeland; and moreover, I did not have to worry about getting my own meals, which made a holiday in itself.

A few years before my first grouse season in Swaledale my employer had grown so lame that he had to be taken to the butts in a sledge. Most men would have given up shoot-ing in the face of such difficulties, but not him. He got into his sledge at the edge of the moor, and a pony, sometimes two ponies, if the track were steep, took him right to his appointed butt. No matter if he had got a somewhat in-accessible butt, he would not change with another gun. On he would go, and if the last few yards were too treacherous for the pony, he got out and walked. One admired his ten-acity of purpose.

In the butt he sat on a specially designed chair, which
allowed him to swivel right round, if the need arose, when
he was shooting. A spring arrangement also permitted him
to lean well back, when he was taking an overhead shot.
And he shot well with all his handicaps. Unlike many
shooting men, my employer always liked me to indicate
where approaching birds were. I had to be very accurate,
too. He did not, however, like to be warned of approaching
birds by the gun in the next butt. I have seen him rather
wroth when a neighbour persisted in shouting, 'Coming to
you.' One gun nearly drove him crazy by shouting, 'Over,'
a dozen times during a drive. He particularly detested
'Over,' and I will say that it is a maddening call, especially
if you have seen the bird or birds a minute before the
caller. Anyone who committed that breach of etiquette was
in danger of not appearing on the moor again.

It was very pleasant to be in those Swaledale moor butts
on a lovely August or September day. I would load my
guns, and lean back on the turf coping until the birds
started to wheel on the horizon, then I would straighten,
and keep a look-out for the vanguard. If the horizon were a
considerable distance off, the grouse would often settle
a long way in front of the butts. Covey after covey would
appear without a bird getting as far as the butts. Then the
beaters would come in view as mere specks. They would
dip below the skyline again, and be lost in the darkness of
the heather, except perhaps for their white flags. These flags
by the way, become dingier and dingier as the season advances until they are nearly as dark as the heather. Suddenly
there would be a vigorous flag-wagging, a sign that grouse
had been raised. A moment or two later one would detect
them skimming over the heather in the direction of the
butts. Another moment or two and they were against the
blue sky, heading the right way ; or if they were inclined to
break, a flanker would rise from a peat hag, and give his
flag a few waves. If they were not coming to our butt, I
would watch the performance of the other guns. I would

note how the known duds consistently upheld their reputations for missing, and how the cracks consistently upheld their reputations for bringing down their grouse from any angle or from any height, if the birds were in shot at all. As the beaters came nearer, there would be a continuous volleying all along the line of butts. I have seen the air full of grouse on those Swaledale moors, some flying forward, some flying back, and some flying out over the flankers. I remember one drive at Swinnergill ; it was a terrific cannonade. Never have I seen so many grouse in the air at one time as I saw there. It was a hot time for the loaders. I always took two full bags of cartridges to each drive, if possible, and I was glad that I had them there. One reason why I always took so many cartridges with me was because people who happened to run out of ammunition during a drive invariably came to my employer for a loan ; and he always gave them a loan. Therefore, I liked to feel that I could meet any eventuality, although I was sometimes chaffed for my excessive caution.

When a grouse drive is over, there is a scattering of guns and loaders and dogs to pick up the fallen. A lot of jealousy is apparent at that function often. A man hates to see another pick up the birds that he has shot with so much difficulty. They all go into the same panniers, and they all belong to one man really, the owner of the shoot, but, nevertheless, I have heard guns speak sharply to each other when a bird has been wrongly picked. I used to marvel at this seeming childishness, but when I began to shoot a lot of grouse myself at the beginning of the war, I hated to see my neighbour, maybe a bungler, walk out coolly and lift birds that I had shot. Some of those bunglers grow cunning in their endeavours to prove that they are not bunglers. Grouse have a habit of carrying on a long way after they have been hard hit, then suddenly they drop stone dead. The bungler marks those, and makes off for them, hoping that no one else has seen them die. I know several 'sportsmen' who augment their kills in that fashion.

They are all keepers or farmers. The upper-class gun has little chance of adding to his bag by marking birds that have dropped a long way behind. For one thing there are too many sharp-eyed people about when he is shooting. For another, there is more discipline. Guns are not usually allowed to wander far behind the butts, because they might disturb the next drive. Grouse are often driven all day to the same row of butts. I used to marvel at that. Being accustomed to pheasants, I thought that the last drive to the same butts was bound to be a failure, but actually the last drive is often better than the first. As the season advances, grouse do get wary, and will avoid a place where they have always met with a hot reception, but they are slow to learn.

If the upper-class poaching gun cannot gather birds far behind the butts that someone else has shot, he can often amass a fair heap of birds after a drive by going at once as near his neighbours butt as he dare to pick up all the doubtful birds possible, and as many as he can of those that are not doubtful. So eager is he that he will many a time leave birds lying unpicked against his own butt .That type of gun is generally well-known to the rest of the team. His avaticiousness loses him many a grouse that he has shot genuinely ; for other guns are apt to retaliate by picking all they can near his butt for a start. On the whole, the greedy gun is a nuisance on a moor. He causes endless confusion. Men and dogs spend hours looking for grouse that he has lifted ; and grouse are left lying in the heather, because the neighbouring guns assume that he has gathered them.

On the day after a big grouse shoot a couple or three keepers, perhaps with a dale farmer to carry part of the bag, scour the moor at each side of the butts with their dogs. Incredible quantities of dead and wounded grouse are often picked up. Some may be lying half a mile from the butts ; others may be lying hard against them, and occasionally a heap is found lying on a butt coping that a careless pannier-pony man has missed. One keeper had a cast-iron system for preventing that. He made the pannier men mark the quantity of grouse picked at each butt in a note-book. I daresay that the pannier men found their clerical work a bit of a nuisance, but the book definitely showed that they had visited every butt or otherwise, and it was easy to count the bag at the end of the day without handling all the grouse.

I often went with the moor keepers to pick up after a shoot ; in fact, I always went, unless another shoot were fixed for that day. In that case, loading was the priority job. Fifteen and twenty brace of grouse were common figures for a pick-up. Once, I believe we got twenty-five brace, a day's bag for many a small moor.

We usually took our guns to the pick-up to finish off wounded birds, and one might be forgiven for thinking that we added to the pick-up by shooting a few grouse that were not wounded, but actually I never saw any keeper try to knock down a sound bird. More than that, I seldom saw a wounded grouse that needed a shot. The dogs generally were able to cope with them unaided. So our pick-up bag was a true indication of the amount of game that can be left on a moor after a shoot.

One fact that always struck me on those pick-up days was the comparative scarcity of grouse coveys. On the previous day when the shoot was in progress there might have been thousands of grouse over the butts, and the impression that one got was that the whole moor was swarming. A green-horn could easily have imagined that he could make a bee-line across any part of the moor and let off his gun every ten yards or so. But even in the most bumper seasons there are parts of the moor that hardly hold any birds. When one considers that perhaps two miles, or even more, are taken in at one drive, the multitude of grouse at the butts is easily explained. And when one considers also that the return drive is augmented by the birds that have gone over un-scathed from the first drive, the origin of the vast packs is still more easily comprehended. The second drive may show the grouse population on four, or five, or even six square miles of moorland. So it was small wonder that we usually saw only a few grouse on pick-up days.

Of course, there are areas on every good moor that might be classed as densely-populated with grouse. These areas are the places where feed is good and plentiful. I remember one such place near the edge of the moor barely a mile from the Lodge. It was a long, low ridge. The heather on it was short, and, I suppose, sweet to the grouse palate ; for there were always birds about it in the afternoons.

The butts on those Swaledale moors are for the greater part substantial structures. They are circular mainly, and built of stone, millstone grit, I believe. The circular form allows of a drive from both sides. The entry is narrow, which prevents sheep from taking up their abode inside. Such butts require little attention. Fresh sods are laid on the coping a week or two before the Twelfth, and a stone or two may have to be re-built, but generally speaking those Swaledale grouse butts are everlasting.

Those moorland keepers build their own butts. No skilled mason is needed ; and the workmanship could shame many a man who calls himself a skilled mason. I daresay that the art of drystone walling has been handed down from father to son in the dale for hundreds of years, and the keepers are, or were, nearly all dalesmen. Those miles of wall in Swaledale testify that the inhabitants are, and were, a race of stone masons. Many a time when I have been struggling over one six foot wall after another on Mukerside, I have wished that the art had not been quite so popular.

At a few places, very few, the butts are made of wood, and only serve one drive. Originally, I suppose that they were put up to try a new drive, but they remain. They are quite as good as the stone butts, although they seem conspicuous and out of place in a wilderness. The floors of those butts were also wooden. On a wet day they became slippery, and one had to be careful. The stone butts had concrete floors, which was a decided advantage.

At Swinnergill, where we stood in wooden butts, I saw a

gun miss forty-two consecutive shots. It seems rather incredible, especially when one considers that the gun was
usually a good shot. The air was black with grouse for half
an hour before the drive finished, and he banged away
without effect. At least, there was no effect on the grouse,
but there was a marked effect on his temper. He grew more
and more annoyed, until he was practically boiling with
rage. When the drive finished, he fired a shot at the wooden
butt to test the cartridges, but I cannot remember whether
it was really proved that they were at fault. Probably excitement had more to do with his bad shooting than faulty
cartridges. When he got to the tenth miss or so, he would be
so peeved that he would fire at random. Cartridges certainly
do vary, but I think that forty-two successive duds is
hardly a possibility. At any rate he hit the butt; so there
was a morsel of comfort in that.

Twice I have seen shooting accidents. Both were on the
moors, but luckily they were not serious. The first involved
a loader, who was in the butt with his boss. A pellet struck
him on one cheek just below the eye. It penetrated fairly
deeply, and bled profusely. The man was considerably
shaken. I think he imagined what might have happened if
the pellet had struck an eye. That frightened him more than
the actual pain, although he probably had some of that, too.
Nobody took the blame for the accident. The next gun was
not guilty, because he had not fired then. Therefore, it must
have been a gun farther off. In that case, one can hardly
imagine that a dropping pellet could have had so much
penetration. However, the fact remains that the loader had a
pellet in his face, and has it probably to this day. He went
to the doctor that same night, but the pellet was not
extracted.

A season or two later I saw a keeper get hit as he was
bringing in the drive. I saw the man pull out his handker-
chief suddenly and press it to his face, but he did not stop
more than a second or two. He must have been slightly
tougher than the loader, because he had several wounds

when he got to the butts. One hand had been hit as well as his face. Often I have wondered why more keepers or beaters are not hit. Grouse that fly low towards the guns when the drive is nearly in are a potential danger always. I have seen shots fired at them that must have been near someone. Only the fact that a charge of No. 6 shot loses velocity quickly can account for some apparently miraculous escapes.

I have felt the hot wind from a shot several times, and that is not pleasant. but the nearest I ever came to a direct hit was on Mukerside. We keepers, three of us, were out shooting grouse for the Lodge pot. One keeper acted as beater ; the other one and I did the shooting. Grouse have their favourite lines of flight ; so a fair amount of sport can be got driving with only one beater when those flight lines are known, if the wind is right.

At this particular place on Mukerside there were no butts. We both stood in peat hags, separated by about fifty yards of level moor. Only our heads were visible to each other. It was a lovely day. I watched the cloud shadows trail over the heather on the far side of the dale, and was dreaming happy day-dre ms, when a grouse came whirring round the shoulder of a knoll in front of us. It was only flying a yard from the ground. I eased my gun to the ready position, but the bird seemed to be making a better shot for the other keeper ; so I let him take it. On it came, rocking and skimming alternately, towards my right. Then, as it reached a point almost in line between the two peat hags, I saw the barrels of my mate's gun pointing in my direction. In a flash I realised that he was going to fire, but I had no time to duck. Bang ! went the shot. Almost immediately I felt something hit the little finger of my right hand, which was raised then above the hag. There was no blood, only a dark mark where the pellet had bounced off the skin. I was fortunate. If the grouse had been two yards above the heather, I might have got the whole charge. Several pellets did whistle past me, but only one hit was registered.

XIII. A well camouflaged butt, half stone, half peat sods

XIV. Relaxation in a covert camp.

XV. A genial old dalesman

XVI. Sunset on Skiddaw

One old gentleman that I remember well used to be so frightened that he would follow his birds in line with the other guns that he carried two triangular wooden affairs with him always, which the loader had to erect on each side of the butt before the beginning of a drive. Whether he had ever caused an accident or not I never knew, but he always had his guards up. And they certainly did prevent him from pointing his gun along the line, when following a bird. Usually, however, the man who shoots a lot gets an instinct that prevents him from shooting dangerously. Unconsciously he defines the arc inside which he must not shoot. When he reaches the forward limit of it, he raises his gun, then carries on behind.

That careful, old shooter had a very slightly-built loader, who was good at his job, but who had a habit of putting his guns and cartridges into the lunch cart to save him the bother of carrying them. One could hardly blame him ; he was small, and the way was often long and rough. Usually the lunch cart went up towards the butts, or beyond them ; but one day we unexpectedly started at a line of butts which were seldom used, and where there was no lunch hut. It was arranged that we would move up to the main butts, nearly a mile away, after that one drive. The lunch cart, of course, went on its own way, taking the little loader's gear with it. If the little man hadn't been so far in the rear, he might have noticed that ; but only when the drive was about to begin did he find out that his guns were missing. Great consternation ! The old gentleman got the loan of a gun from one of the other guests, and the little loader hurried off to the distant lunch hut for the missing pair. Actually he might as well have stopped at the lunch hut, because we were going quite near to it afterwards, but back he came with the missing guns. And to save time he walked straight through the part of the moor reserved for the second drive. To crown all he hove in sight when the first drive was nearly in, and probably turned a covey or two back. The shooting men were not at all amused, but nothing was said

J

directly to the little loader. Probably most of us would take the shortest cut in a similar situation. We would, however, try to be less conspicuous.

The old gentleman of the missing guns met his end at the beginning of the war bravely by enemy action. He was, as far as I could learn, on his yacht off the South Coast when a Nazi aircraft came over and machine-gunned him. He was a game, old chap to be afloat at such a time. It was with regret that I saw the notice of his death in *The Times*.

The guests who came to the Lodge for the first two or three weeks of the season were generally first-class shots. With them we got good bags of grouse. The best bag in my time was nearly four hundred brace, but five hundred brace bags have been made on those moors quite often. A two hundred brace day was common, and when we got down to a hundred brace per day, we thought we were doing only very moderately.

When I first went to the moors, the grouse that were shot at the top end of the dale were left with the keeper there for despatch. Latterly all the grouse were taken to the larder at the Lodge. That meant more work for me, and incidentally for another two keepers. We were at it early in the morning and late at night often. In the evening the heap of grouse on the larder floor had to be tediously separated into young and old, then hung up. In the morning they had to be packed into hampers for the gamedealers, and into one brace and two brace cardboard boxes for presents. Then all had to be booked accurately. It was a busy time when two or three hundred brace of birds had to be handled. One could not afford to spend much time on individual grouse when separating the young from the old ; so I merely tested the hardness or otherwise of the skull with my right thumb. It is a certain test at the beginning of the season, but towards the end the young birds often have skulls almost as hard as their elders. Some keepers study the wing feathers, some test the beak; but these are slower methods. Often after I have graded several hundred grouse my thumb has been extremely sore. The skulls of some of the old cock grouse were like marbles in their hardness. In pre-war days there was a considerable difference between the price of a young and an old grouse ; so it was essential to separate them properly. A well-cooked young grouse is an epicure's dish, but an old one, however well-cooked, has a bitterish flavour.

To avoid errors in packing we never threw more grouse on the floor than one hamper would hold. The capacity of a hamper is fairly consistent. To avoid error still further the birds were packed with the same number in each row. Thus, if a grouse were lying on the floor after the hamper had been packed, we knew that something was wrong. A chit was enclosed with the number, and the hamper was tied up and sealed. I could never understand why seals were used, but used they were. We sent away thousands of pheasants without seals on the hampers and I never heard of any going astray. During the war, however, many a cardboard container arrived at its destination empty, and these containers were more secure than the hampers, which could be opened by cutting a string.

After a busy morning in the game larder I was always ready for breakfast. I got that in the servants' hall, and it was a substantial affair. Before I finished, the first loaders were rolling up, and when I got out to the gun-room, I usually found a hive of industry. Gun cases were open on the bench, which ran round three sides of the gun-room, and the loaders were wiping the oil from their weapons. A lot of oil is used in that manner for little purpose. Nearly every loader smears his guns, after they are cleaned, with a copious dose of oil, even when the day has been dry and perhaps sunny. Next morning the oil comes off into a rag. It would have been better in the bottle.

While the guns and cartridges were being made ready, a big cattle wagon would arrive at the gun-room door. Gradually it received a load of gear : lunch baskets, cartridge bags and magazines, mackintosh bags, shooting seat ;

then lastly dogs, keepers and loaders. During the war the guests travelled in it also, but in pre-war days they went to the moor in state. They had limousines, Rolls Royces, Bentleys and I don't know what. Anyway, we got away from the gun-room, and finally were dumped with our chattels three, four, five or even six miles from the Lodge as the crow flies. A detour by the village made the distance greater, and I believe that the farthest-out stopping place required a journey of twelve miles by road. If we happened to be taking a few beaters with us also, the drive was relieved of its tedium by a choir on the roof of the cabin. Some of those lads had excellent voices. They chortled away for miles, although their seat was rather a cold one on a crisp autumn morning. Whenever possible I went on to the roof with them, but I did not do so for musical reasons. It was the only place, excepting the driver's cabin, where I was certain of not becoming sick. There was plenty of fresh air on top, and the swaying of the wagon was not quite so pronounced. Lots of people could not stand the journey inside. The exhalations of closely packed men and dogs, the tobacco fumes, and the rocking motion was too much for queasy stomachs. I noticed, rather strangely, that healthy, never-ill persons were first to be affected in the wagon. Probably their more delicate mechanism gave them warning first that they were being poisoned.

It was a bad day, indeed, if we could not go shooting. Heavy rain was quite often ignored, but a thick mist could cancel all arrangements. Birds will not drive well when the moors are obscured. They fly anywhere, because they cannot tell where the beaters are. In addition to that, there is an element of danger both to beaters and shooters, when a thick mist is lying on the moors. Beaters get out of touch with each other, and wander anywhere. Sometimes they don't get the starting signal; so they stand for hours, unaware that some of their mates have gone. I have seen confusion now and then, when mist has descended unexpectedly on a shooting party; and I remember how disappointed the guns once were when they abandoned a shoot for mist, then found a glorious sunny day as they neared the Lodge. The mist was confined to the higher parts of the moor, and had never obscured the dale at any time during the day. That sort of happening is a sore disappointment to the rabid shooting man. He is liable to moan about it for years.

On the days when the guests were not shooting I often went out with the keepers to shoot snipe, golden plover, or blackgame. The snipe haunted the reedy patches on the Pastures, or the soggy, lower slopes of Mukerside. They were good sport. On windy days they took a lot of hitting.

The golden plover used to stand about on the Pastures near the Lodge. When I went over to the moors first, they were in considerable numbers, but latterly they dwindled for some unknown reason. A single bird was not easy to hit, but I am afraid that a shot was occasionally fired at the mass. I have often seen several plover killed with one shot, but I will say that it is difficult to single a plover out of a densely wheeling pack, or congregation. I think, by the way, that 'congregation' is the correct technical term for a mass of golden plover. The shooting of plover gave me little pleasure. They are rather nice birds, and their plaintive note on the moors in a swirling mist is somewhat saddening.

As for blackgame, I don't ever want to shoot another. These handsome birds seem to be a dying race. They can be very hard to hit, if they are flying high, or if they are swinging down a hillside, but, nevertheless, their numbers seem to decrease year by year. And that remark can be applied to the whole country, if all that I read about black-game be true.

The last blackgame I shot, and probably the last I will ever shoot, was among the pastures opposite the village of Muker. I was detailed to go to a certain place behind one of those numerous stone walls. Another keeper was below me, and a keeper was driving. I went up behind the wall cautiously to my stand, taking a peep now and then over the coping. Exactly opposite where I intended to stand, about fifty yards into the pasture, was a thorn bush. On the bush, eating the berries, were three blackgame birds. They were rather too wide for a shot ; so I contented myself with having a look at them from between two stones on the wall top. They were quite unaware of my presence. Far off I heard a shot occasionally, as the driving keeper advanced. He was probably shooting at rabbits, as no blackgame came forward. At length he appeared over the opposite wall of the pasture. The blackgame took to flight at once, and I dropped the nearest. It was a greyhen, which annoyed me considerably. When I showed my kill to the keeper down the wall, he was pleased that the drive had not been blank, but I felt that I had shot enough blackgame to satisfy me for some time.

Sometimes in our peregrinations we would fall in with a covey of partridges. We usually tried to add some of them to the bag. Once I added a brace to the bag unwittingly. Among my jobs was the important one of providing the Lodge with rabbits ; so I set off one afternoon in August to get a few for the pot. There were masses of rabbits about a mile updale from the Lodge on the side of Ivelet Pasture. I walked through some rushes, and a rabbit broke cover in front of me. It provided a broadside shot, as it was trying to get to the burrow at the far side of a barish patch. I fired and the cony turned a somersault dead. At the same time a covey of partridges went chirping away from around the rabbit. They were absolutely invisible to me when I let my gun off, although the grass was so short that one would have thought that a mouse could hardly have found concealment in it. When I went forward to bag my kill, two young partridges were lying dead nearby. I was in a bit of a funk. The partridge season had not opened, and I was not sure that my employer would accept my story. However, I took the birds to the Lodge. Later, a message was brought to me by one of the indoor staff to the effect that I had to shoot my next batch of rabbits up by Ivelet Pasture.

As I have already said, I shot a lot of grouse at the beginning of the war, when the usual guests were not available. These were hard days. We carried all our grouse ourselves off the moor, and on hot days that was no fun. If we were shooting at the top of the dale, we had perhaps three miles to tramp before we got to the bus terminus at Keld. Then when we got off at Oxnop Bridge, we had a stiff pull up to the Lodge. That last half mile tested our powers of endurance to the utmost. I don't know what the gradient is between the Swale river and the Lodge, but it looked to me often like the slope of a house roof. There was one compensation. When we got to the top, we were generally in time for a cup of tea.

In pre-war days I occasionally played the pipes on the terrace in front of the Lodge during dinner. When I was first asked to do that I was somewhat nervous. The pipes had not been played on for a week or two, and the bag and reeds were, therefore, dry. A pipe bag has to be moist, otherwise it will not hold in air properly ; and dry reeds are harsh, if they play at all. On the other hand, wet reeds are apt to stop also. They are temperamental things are pipes, and only go well if they are played often, but not for long at a time. So, my pipes were out of order when I was first asked to play outside the Lodge dining-room. However, I spent an hour with them before the appointed time, and I did manage to get them going fairly well. Then I blew them up in front of the kitchen, and marched boldly round to the dining-room window. I played perhaps a quarter of an hour. Luckily, I did not see the housemaids leaning out from a upstairs window. Nor did I see the penny which one of them threw down on to the flagstones in front of me. If I had seen all that, I might have bungled my job. As things were, I made no mistakes, at least, none that would have been apparent to the Sassenach ear, and I was rattling away at 'The Highland Wedding' when the butler came out with a note of thanks for me. The guests had enjoyed my piping, I gathered. The note was written on a menu card. I still have it somewhere, I think. If I had been a boozer, my employer would have invited me in for a glass of wine, but he knew my inclinations, and let me depart in peace. Only on the very last time I played did he ask me to have a drink, and I accepted. The liquor was sherry, if I remember rightly. I played to him and two friends then. They sat in the drawing-room. One of the friends was a Scot. He was also a connoisseur of pipe music, and he selected the tunes. Three that I remember were, 'John MacDonald of Glencoe', 'Blair Drummond' and 'Duntroon'. They are respectively, march, strathspey and reel, and are not tunes that the average person knows. I believe that the Scottish guest had spent some of his time in the Lovat Scouts ; so that would account for his knowledge of pipe music.

Once or twice I played for the staff, when there were no guests in the Lodge. The housekeeper was very fond of the pipes. She told me once that she knew Pipe-Major Ross, probably the most successful piper of the last thirty or forty years ; so she had heard good piping. One of the kitchen staff also had a leaning towards the Piobaireachd. I was, therefore, assured of an appreciative audience, and that helps one to play well. Actually, I have found that the pipes are appreciated in England quite as much as in Scotland. The English people may not be able to tell one tune from another, but they are thrilled by the martial clamour. And there was a clamour when I played in that restricted back passage of the Lodge. As I marched backwards and forwards, I myself felt the savage beat of the notes in the confined space.

As October advanced, and the autumn tints began to appear in the gills, my thoughts turned again to the hut in the Lake District. The bags of grouse dwindled then, and one began to feel that something was over. The warmth and hopefulness of August was only a happy memory. One day we would go out for the last shoot of the season. On the following day I would give the guns an extra oiling and packing. Cartridges were stowed away in their original cases. Everything was made ready for departure. I always had a feeling of flatness between those few days between the end of the shooting and the exodus. One morning my employer would go. The staff would wave farewell as his car vanished round the gun-room corner. That was the first break-up. Probably the following morning the shooting-brake would come round to the front of the Lodge. A load of gear would be put into it for delivery at the Lakeland residence. My chattels went in with the rest, and finally, I climbed aboard with the chauffeur. We were off. Down to the village we would go, turn right, cross the Swale bridge, then make updale. As we passed the hamlet of Satron, we would look across to the Lodge, high up on the hillside to our right, and we would see a white tablecloth waving at the kitchen door. That was our good-bye. After that we bowled rapidly to the head of the dale. We usually stopped at Keld to see the keeper there; then over Tail Bridge, down steeply to Kirkby Stephen, on to Appleby and Penrith to the Lakeland.

As we neared Keswick, and the jumbled mass of the fells appeared, often with the gold and crimson beauty of sunset on them, straight in front of us, and the valleys filled with pearly mist, I got a thrill of pleasure that cannot be described by mere words. On our left the Vale of St. John blazed with the rich, warm colours of autumn, and on our right was the slaty-blue summit of Saddleback, usually clearly-defined and serene against the evening sky. I love that view of Derwent Vale from the road this side of Threlkeld at any time. When I used to see it after an absence of three months in Swaledale, I thought it was the loveliest sight on earth.

Gradually that panorama was lost as we entered Keswick, but another, more intimate view unfolded when we left it. I was almost on my own terrain. At Ullock Moss, a quarter of a mile beyond Portinscale, I felt that I was really coming home. There the estate began.

At the signpost above Little Braithwaite Farm I took my tackle out of the brake, shook hands with the driver, who was only a temporary man, then I went twenty yards up the Newlands Valley road to the gateway, which is the entrance to this wood. As I staggered up the pathway, I noted the changes that had taken place during my short absence. There was an air of desolation hanging over the glade. The erstwhile golden ragwort was no more than withered stalks ; the bracken was tinged here and there with red and yellow, and the deciduous trees had on them a hint of the approaching winter. As I fumbled for the key of the hut door, I noticed that there were cobwebs in the keyhole and between the jambs and the door. Obviously no one had been inside during my sojourn in Swaledale. I found the key at length, probably in the fourth pocket that I tried ; I inserted it among the cobwebs, turned it, pressed the latch, and I was again in the old abode. An air of dampness and decay usually greeted me. Soot had fallen down the chimney, and lay at the back of the fireplace, which showed patches of rust here and there. There was dust on everything. How it got inside I never could tell. In the grate were the ashes of the papers that I had burned on the morning of my departure. Sometimes there was evidence that rats had found an entry. Once there was damage by mice. A cushion was gnawed in several places. In later years I always laid enough poison inside the hut to kill off any rodents before they did me any damage while I was away. That stopped the nuisance. I invariably left dry sticks in the oven in case I returned on a rainy day, but they were damp, too. However, they did make a blaze, if I put a shower of paraffin over them. Then I heaped on the coal, so that I might have a big enough fire to dry the place and my bedding before night. There was never any water at hand ; so I took the bucket along to the spring. When I got back I filled the kettle, and in less than a quarter of an hour I was sitting down to a feed. The housekeeper at the Lodge always sent me off with a box of provisions, which was very thoughtful of her. I had food for several days, even if I did not see my grocei. And it was pleasant to sit by the window drinking tea while the shadows fell in the glade. I saw the rabbits emerge from the edge of the wood, and perhaps I would hear a cock pheasant go noisily to his roost among the larches. Then I pulled my bedding through into the kitchen. Steam rose from it, but soon that ceased. The hut was gradually becoming more like a home. About ten p.m. I made up the bed. A few minutes later I was between the sheets watching the dancing firelight on the wall and thinking of the moors that I had left. Thus I returned to the hut.

V. MEDLEY

Peace   *Shooting*   *Gamekeeping To-day*
Miscellany   *Living in a Hut*   *Piping*
Epilogue

I DO not own a wireless set; so when peace came to Europe after long, agonizing years of war, I was caught unprepared. I knew, of course, that peace was imminent, but even that did not lessen my surprise and gladness.

On the evening of May 7th, 1945, I went out at dusk to have a wander round the knoll at the end of the wood, which is an intake of Braithwaite Lodge Farm. When I got over the wood fence into Charlie Relph's intake, I saw the Back Howe ablaze straight above the village. It was obvious that whins were burning, and I could hear a lot of shouting. As I stood on the green pathway, looking at the glow against the dark background of mountain and wood, the farmer himself appeared from the direction of the Lodge. He stopped some distance from me, and gazed as if he were hypnotized at the fire. Even then I did not realise its significance, but I went towards Charlie Relph, and asked what all the commotion was about. He looked at me woodenly for a second or two, and replied that the village youths were probably celebrating Victory. Then I knew that the war in Europe was over, the war that had often seemed endless. The glad news had come over on the radio only a few minutes previously. A formal announcement was to be made on the morrow by Mr. Churchill. It was a memorable night. While we stood there in the twilight discussing the German debacle, another fire started halfway up on the breast of Skiddaw at the other side of the valley. I went back to the hut, thinking deeply, and before I went to bed, I played a few tunes on the pipes. When I stopped, I heard someone shouting my name down near Ullock. It was a calm, balmy night.

Next morning the bells of Crosthwaite were ringing out a message of peace and hope. It was a very lovely day, and that message tolled through the sunny valley like a benison. Three-quarters of a mile away, and visible from the hut door, a Red Ensign was waving over the village sports ground. The little birds sang in the trees beside the hut, and down near the fence three hawthorn bushes were in blossom. They seemed to symbolize Equality, Fraternity and Liberty.

In the forenoon I walked across to the Kennels to feed my ferrets. At Swinside between the farm and the inn there were masses of streamers over the roadway ; and Swinside Lodge boarding-house farther on was festooned also with streamers. From a pole in front of the house waved a Union Jack.

In the afternoon I heard hunting hollas all over the valley. People were on holiday. The hollas started at Ullock, and were echoed from the village. On Barrow I saw the mass of a potential bonfire. It stood on the Round Man, which is about halfway up. On the highridge two Union Jacks were waving, and another floated above the pile of sticks on the Round Man. After an early dinner I climbed up through the wood on to the fell. It was hot in the wood, but a cooling breeze blew on the highridge.

At the pile of sticks, which the Scouts had got in this wood, Alan Gould, a village boy, stood guard. He told me that some boys were off for more sticks. We sat down together on the slope that faces Derwent Valley. We chatted a bit, then I took out my monocular to see how much bunting and flags I could see. There was a slight haze in the valley, but signs of Victory celebrations were evident from Thornthwaite to Keswick. Two ladies came up to see what was to be seen. They did not stop long. Then a crowd of soldiers and village girls arrived. The soldiers were carrying old car tyres for the bonfire. They were sweating

with the long pull uphill. Everybody sat down on the
Round Man, and surveyed the glorious, sunny panorama
below them. It was a day to remember. Even now I see
that happy gathering on Barrow Fell, and the village below,
festooned with flags and gay bunting, and farther off, the
blueness of Bassenthwaite Lake. Such days occur only once
or twice in a lifetime.

I did not see the bonfire lit that night, because I went
along to Thornthwaite to a little party with some friends
who live there. They are Czechs, and they know how to
enjoy themselves. While we were sitting after supper discussing the wonderful news, the lady next door brought in
glasses of port, and we drank to a long peace in Europe.
There was still war in the Far East, but one felt that the end
of it could not be long delayed.

The first intimation that Japan was preparing to surrender
came to me one sunny day about two o'clock in the afternoon. I was biking my way towards the Kennels when I
met Billy Gilpin, the roadman, down there near the beck
bridge. He told me that Japan had collapsed. Someone
had heard it on the one o'clock news. I was elated, but I
could not understand why Japan should give in so easily.
Certainly she had been frightened by a couple of atomic
bombs, but no Allied troops were on her soil. Later in the
afternoon I asked several people if they had heard of Japan's
surrender. They all confirmed Billy's statement, with the
qualification that the terms had not actually been accepted.
So a couple of days passed in uncertainty. On Sunday,
August 12th, I was climbing Maiden Moor with little
Miss J. It was an ideal day for climbing, clear and sunny,
but not too hot. As we reached the saddle top between
Catbells and Maiden Moor, we found a home-made pennant
fluttering from a cairn of rocks. On the lower half of it was
a rough representation of the Japanese flag. Above that was
written V.F.E. Day, Aug. 10th, 1945. The initials obviously
stood for Victory in the Far East. All this was done in red
ink on a white rag. Miss J. asked me what V.F.E. stood for,

and I gravely replied that it meant Victory For Ever. When I said that I hoped that my statement might be right. There was still uncertainty as to whether the Far East war was finished or not, but that pennant assured me that most people believed that the end was really in sight. So I climbed the fell even more happily than before. We sat for a few moments on the summit, and looked down on the lovely face of Derwentwater, which was entrancingly serene that afternoon. Then we climbed again. Halfway up the plateau of Maiden Moor we passed a band of youths resting on the sward. We exchanged greetings, and carried on. Our objective was the highest point on Maiden Moor. At the cairn of stones on Gate Crag we assumed that we had reached it, but just to make certain, we went to a cairn farther on. On each of those cairns we placed a stone, and thereby made the summit two inches higher. Down in Borrowdale near Stonethwaite we saw a camp of white tents. People were beginning to relax after the long years of war. It was a perfect afternoon.

Not until three days later, however, did the official news of Japan's surrender come over the radio. That was on August 15th, 1945. I got my first inkling of it as I was passing Swinside Lodge that morning. Two men and some children, all visitors, were marching in front of the house, carrying British, American and Russian flags. As they marched, they sang 'John Brown's Body.'

While I was watching the procession, young John Thwaite from up the valley came down the road on his bike. He stopped, and like me, he watched the fun. I suspected that the war was really over, but I asked him to make certain, and I learned that the Prime Minister had announced the surrender of Japan immediately after the midnight broadcast. As we stood there talking over the glad tidings, the visitors at the Lodge began to hang out bunting. In a few minutes the front of the house was festooned with flags. And that was how I knew that peace had arrived.

On my way back to the hut I walked across the beck, which was very low, to carry the news to the Sea Scouts who were camping there then. As I approached, no signs of life were visible around the tents, but the boys were inside, playing some sort of game. A drizzle of rain was beginning to fall then ; so I went inside also, and told them the news. They were delighted. Some of them wished that they were back in Liverpool for the celebrations ; others were quite glad to celebrate in the camp.

In the evening I went over to the Big House. It was my day for delivering rabbits there, and although it was a general holiday, I did my usual necessary jobs. After I had skinned the rabbits I went into the housekeeper's room to hear the King's speech. It came over the radio at nine o'clock. Then the housekeeper produced a bottle of port wine, and the half dozen of us who were present drank a glass each. It was about eleven o'clock when I left the Big House, but rockets were going off everywhere around then. Undoubtedly it was a great night.

The following night there was another bonfire on Barrow Fell. The village Scouts had dragged up wood in the afternoon. A good crowd was gathered on the fell at dusk, and I was a unit in it. When darkness had finally descended, the pile of sticks was lit. It was a glorious blaze. It lit up all the people sitting and standing in the bracken around it. There was some singing, and fireworks were let off. Across the valley another fire blazed up on Latrigg. It was even bigger than ours. I should say that something more combustible than wood was used. Then rockets were fired all over Keswick. They appeared to us on the felltop as shooting stars. Then as our fire began to wane, another two flared up in the darkness far off. One was down the valley beyond Bassenthwaite. The other was at the far side of Derwentwater, somewhere near Lodore. Later, towards midnight, the crowd that had watched the fire on Barrow Fell above the hut danced on the bridge in the middle of the village to the strains of Corporal Jimmy Rutland's accordion.

I did not dance, but I watched the fun. It was in full swing when I made my way up the lonning for some supper, and even after that I heard music. I remember that I stepped outside before I went to bed. The sky was starry and the music came now and then on the light breeze.

Shooting

The art of shooting with a shotgun cannot really be learned from any book, but a few bookish hints may help the practical work. To be a good shot I think that good health is of prime importance. The second essential is a fair amount of physical strength, but it is not necessary that one be a Samson. An active man who is not muscle-bound fills the second requirement. Great brain-power is not necessary, but the shooter must have a decisive mind. 'He who hesitates is lost' is an axiom that applies to shooting with the shotgun.

In the actual practice of shooting the first essential is probably good balance, which means that the feet must be in a certain position immediately before a shot is fired. That position varies slightly with individual shooters, but broadly speaking, the feet must be apart ; and if the shooter fires from the right shoulder, the left foot ought to be in front of the right. I have seen inexperienced shooters waiting for a shot with their feet in the military 'attention' position. They are lost if any sudden swing has to be made either to the right or left.

The gun, while one is waiting, should be nearly horizontal ; the top of the stock heel somewhere about the right elbow, and the left hand grasping the fore-end of the gun not too far back, otherwise one loses a certain amount of control over the weapon. Some shooters, if they be long in the arm, use a grip that slides on to the barrels. That enables them to grasp the gun farther forward than is normal. Personally, I grasp the fore-end well forward, but I do grasp the wood, and not the metal.

K

When taking a low shot, such as a rabbit presents, the weight will incline to the left foot ; and when one is taking, say, a high overhead pheasant, the weight will incline to the right foot. The expert shot, even when he is walking through rough undercover, will assume a well-balanced position in a flash. That is mainly why he is an expert shot.

There must be no hesitation when one is about to fire at a moving target, not even the merest fraction of indecision, at the instant of pressing the trigger. The action must be a smooth follow-through. If one can achieve that smooth, unhesitating movement, there is no need for any exaggerated forward allowance. That applies even to the fastest-moving targets. I once heard a keeper say that he gave a covey of partridges, coming with a good wind, a lead of at least eighteen feet, and he killed the last bird. He certainly did not follow-through properly. Instead he must have aimed at his bird, swept forward the gun rapidly for eighteen feet, hesitated a fraction of a second and fired. That hesitation, slight though it may have been, was sufficient to allow the covey to overtake even his exaggerated lead. How do I know that he hesitated ? I know, because I have never fired, as far as I am aware, eighteen feet in front of any moving target, and I can kill a flying bird as well as most people. I once saw an elderly gentleman fire about six feet behind a pheasant which had only just risen, and was, therefore, not flying very fast. He hesitated, undoubtedly. I was almost behind him, and could see the line of his shot fairly distinctly. A good shot would have killed the same bird, which was crossing, by firing only in front of its beak. A great many moderately-paced targets can be hit thus. When I fire at a rabbit, almost at any range, I shoot just in front of it, that is, of course, if it be a crossing shot. A running-away shot needs no lead at all, except that one may raise the gun an inch or two at the moment of firing, if the rabbit is rather wide. A grouse, or a pigeon, broadside on and flying without wind in its tail, can be killed usually with a lead of one to two feet, according to the range. If the range be longish, however, and the bird is being aided by a strong wind, it may be necessary to double the usual lead. Once on Mukerside I was shooting driven grouse from behind a stone wall. A stiff breeze was blowing up the pasture, and the grouse, instead of coming straight at me, flew broadside on at a distance of perhaps forty yards from the wall. I missed a few birds, and was trying to convince myself that they were too far off, when I decided to fire as if I were trying to kill an imaginary grouse in front of the real one. After that I killed quite a lot of birds. They were being hit by the centre of the shot pattern. But only on that occasion and one or two others when I was grouse-shooting have I deliberately tried to fire far in front of my target ; and even then I do not suppose that I ever shot with more than a four or five feet lead. There is another point : The gun muzzle ought to carry on even after the shot has left it. It is impossible to get a real follow-through movement, unless that point is remembered.

Just before the shot is fired, the eyes must be fixed on the target, and they must be kept there until the shot is ready to go. I suppose that one's eyes are not actually on the target at the instant when the powder explodes, if the target be a fast-moving one ; but the interval between the eyes leaving the target to find the apparent point of impact in front of it is so very slight that one is never conscious of it, unless the target be coming directly overhead. That is my experience, at least, because I close the left eye, when I shoot with the shotgun.

The question as to whether it is advisable to close one eye when shooting with a shotgun is one that has caused a lot of arguments, so many that I believe every man ought to please himself. If the left eye be stronger, and one shoots from the right shoulder, it might be advisable to shut the left eye, but otherwise I cannot see that it matters. My employer used to shoot often with both eyes open, and he was a good shot. For all that I know, he may always have shot with both eyes open. It was only occasionally that

I was in a position to see his eyes when he was shooting.

A naturally good shot can shoot well with almost any type of gun. Others are put off if the gun has not got a certain bend at the heel of the stock, or a certain cast-off in the stock in relation to the barrels. It can be taken as a fairly safe guide that a gun suits one, if the eyes can be fixed on a spot on, say, a plain wall, the gun swept up rapidly and fired without hesitation, and the shot pattern lands evenly around the spot. If the shot goes repeatedly high or low, the bend of the stock heel is not suitable.

Personally, I do not attach much importance to cast-off, but I would let every man please himself on that point. The one man who *must* have an exaggerated cast-off gun (unless he decides to shoot from the other shoulder) is he who has lost the sight of an eye. Then he uses what is generally called a cross-eye gun. Those weapons are not beautiful, but they serve their purpose. They have to be carefully watched, however, in the gun-room, if several loaders are working at the table at the same time. They are apt to roll about, and can easily land on the floor.

Nearly all queerly-built guns are made for the upper classes. I did once know a keeper who used a cross-eye gun, because he had lost the sight of an eye in a shooting accident, but I never knew a normal keeper with an exaggeratedly cast-off gun. Usually a keeper is handed any old sort of a gun when he goes to a place, and he is expected to shoot well with it. The man has to fit the gun. I have made myself fit all the weapons I have ever used, except perhaps one. I had to get my cheek pressed so hard into the stock before I could see along the rib that the gun definitely did not suit me. It was only a borrowed gun ; so I didn't try to adjust myself to it, but I daresay I could have got used to it in a week or two. The correct length of stock appears to me to be more important than anything in deciding the fit of a gun. A too-long stock is an insurmountable handicap often.

Sometimes a good shot will shoot badly with a borrowed gun, not because it is grossly unsuitable for him, but because

it has some peculiarity in its make-up which is strange to
him. The rib may be too high, or too low ; the grip may be
thicker than that of his own gun, or the weapon may be
heavier or lighter. The fact that it obtrudes itself on his
consciousness at the critical moment makes him shoot
badly. I suppose that only highly-strung people are affected
by such trivialities, and the better the shot the more likely
is he to be put off by any peculiarity in a borrowed weapon ;
which is, I suppose, tantamount to saying that the best
shots are highly-strung individuals. And that is correct, I
think. The greater the nervous energy the better the shot.
But although the naturally good shot may make a mess
temporarily when he is using a gun which has some peculiarity to which he is not accustomed, yet, with a little
practice, he would eventually shoot as well with it as if he
were using his own gun. He can master those drawbacks.

It is an old excuse of the duffer that the brand of ammunition that he has been missing with was the cause of his
failures ; but actually cartridges do vary. Even cartridges
out of the same box vary. I have proved that times without
number, because I shoot rabbits and vermin sitting, if I
possibly can. Of course, there are times when the most
powerful cartridge will not kill. The animal may be struck
with an average amount of pellets, but if a vital part is not
hit, or no bones are broken severely enough to incapacitate
the animal, then it gets away, even though it may die a few
seconds after it has disappeared. But apart from that, I have
seen conclusive proof on snow that pellets can drop considerably, if they are fired at an object some distance off.
That the fault did not lie with me was proved by the fact
that if I held slightly above the objects (which were carrion
crows, by the way) I killed more often. Yet, before that
fact was impressed on me, I did kill now and then at the
same range by firing directly at the crows, which showed
that an occasional cartridge was powerful enough to make
a good pattern at the same range, which was about fifty
yards. And I noticed that the pattern varied on the snow.

Sometimes there was an even peppering; at other times there were gaps in the pattern that would easily have let a bird the size of a crow escape without a hit. Perhaps my gun was not too good, but that did not alter the fact that if I had been shooting at flying birds, I might have thought that I was off form.

One afternoon many years ago I sat down in a wood near the beckside to wait for a sparrowhawk to return to her nest. My hide was barely thirty yards from the foot of the tree, and the nest was something like fifteen feet up the tree, which was a fir. The hawk came back, and perched beside her nest with her front towards me. I took careful aim, and to my astonishment, the hawk flew away as if she had never been shot at. That decided me not to bother with the nest until she got settled down again; so I went up to the hut, got a cardboard box, and drew the outline of a sparrowhawk on the front of it. Then I set it up a little more than thirty yards from the hut door, and fired as I had fired at the real hawk. When I went to look at the pattern, I was surprised to find it all in the bottom half of the box. If the drawing had been a genuine hawk, it would also have escaped.

On another occasion I shot at a rabbit which was running up into the plantation on this side of Swinside Fell, and I blew the top of its skull completely off. The range was about thirty yards. Obviously that shot had travelled as a solid ball. But despite those remarks about the erratic behaviour of some cartridges, consistently bad shooting is usually the fault of the man who fires the gun. Even the cheapest proprietary ammunition will seldom let one down very badly, if it is stored properly. In fact, ammunition that is stored in extremely dry conditions, or in extremely damp conditions, is apt to give unsatisfactory results when fired. I have had cartridges that went off like dynamite, and I have had others that exploded like squibs. In a few instances I have had cartridges that absolutely refused to fire at all. These grossly abnormal cartridges had been spoiled by bad storage.

Now, a man may be equipped with the best gun and

cartridges procurable, and he may be a fair shot at the shooting school, but he is not, in my opinion, a real hunter until he knows something of woodcraft and fieldcraft. The casual, fashionable shooter who has everything organised for him by a keeper or keepers does not need a great deal of woodcraft ; all that he needs is skill in the actual handling of the gun. In the case of pheasant-shooting, he stands at a numbered stick at the end of a beat, and the birds are driven over him. In fairness to him, I will say that those high pheasants are not easy to kill. Often I have heard ignorant people say that a pheasant must be an easy target, because it is hand-fed and, therefore, semi-tame. But that is by no means a fact. If some of those critics had to bring down high pheasants for their living, their pay-packet would be light. Nevertheless, it is the man who hunts alone who gets the most satisfaction from shooting. He has to develop a cunning to match the cunning of the creatures that he seeks. Everything that he puts into the bag has been worked for. It is the reward of his own skill ; and that, I think, gives a deeper satisfaction than the sharing of the proceeds of a battue ever does.

Of course, on the grouse moor the house-party shooter has to develop some elementary form of cunning, if he wishes to get his share of shooting. He must not be too conspicuous in his butt, that is, he must not be too brightly clad, nor must he move about unnecessarily, especially if the season be getting on. The birds are wary then. They have learned that those moving things in the butts are on the moor for no good purpose, as far as they are concerned. I have heard curses poured secretly on a woman who persisted in gesticulating with a pair of white gloves on, when grouse appeared on the horizon. Blackgame are particularly quick to spot anything unusual in the butts. They clear off then, unless they happen to be swinging down a hillside like rockets.

The fashionable shooter seldom, if ever, develops the degree of cunning that is exercised almost daily by the gamekeeper. He has not the opportunities of developing it, but, as I have already said, he misses the fundamental pleasure of shooting. He is like the man who collects pictures. He gets a lot of fun from his hobby, but the artist gets more.

The routine of an organised pheasant-shooting day does not start when the guns take their stands at the end of the covert. A lot of work has been put in by keepers and beaters before then. As a rule the keeper meets his team of beaters about eight a.m. at an appointed place, and outlying coverts are driven into the main one straightaway. When that is done, the stops are put out to prevent the birds from wandering away again. Too much time ought not to elapse between the placing of the stops and the arrival of the shooting party, as birds are inclined to be restless at that early hour, and they may fly out of the covert, despite the stops. If one cock pheasant goes cackling over the trees towards the open fields, a hundred may follow in one bunch. Meanwhile, the beaters are lined up waiting the word to move, and if the keeper has assistants, he leaves them in charge and goes off himself to place the guns when they arrive. Some lairds see to the placing of the guns themselves, and a starting time is previously agreed on, but the wise keeper never sets off the drive until he is absolutely certain that the shooting team is in position. The shooting team at a big covert shoot includes loaders and dog-men. The latter may stand behind the guns when the shooting is in progress, if there are suitable hiding places ; but sometimes they wait until the drive is finished.

Once he is sure that the shooting team is in position, the keeper starts his beaters. They are instructed to move slowly, to keep in line, and to tap continually with their sticks. Above all they must not shout. That is theory, but in actual practice it is difficult to make beaters do things as they ought to be done. There are invariably irresponsible men among the beaters, who wander behind their mates when the cover is thick, who will shout with excitement at the wrong time, and who will chatter about their own private interests while the birds are streaming between them unheeded. It is a marvel that drives are not ruined more often. If the beaters have enough sense to come out at the end of the covert in some sort of disciplined form-ation, the keeper's reputation does not suffer so much, but if two or three are visible to the waiting guns a quarter of an hour before the others, there is trouble of some sort. The keeper has usually to bear the brunt of it, although it is hardly ever possible for him to supervise beaters in really thick cover. I know how difficult it is to control heedless, wooden-headed beaters.

The last lap of the drive is generally the most critical one. Pheasants have gone forward running, and have found that their way is barred by wire-netting. They will not fly until the beaters are practically on them, and by that time the undercover is a mass of scuttling birds, the accumulation of the greater part of the drive. A foolish beater runs forward out of line to flush some birds on his own. On he presses. A hundred birds rise around him. They do not see the rest of the beaters, but they see the guns ; so they fly back into the wood. The keeper groans. He would be completely justified if he hit the offending beater over the head with his stick, but he grits his teeth and carries on.

Sometimes the main covert is driven blank, instead of to guns, then the birds are driven home again over guns. The pheasants make good shooting when this method is adopted, particularly if they have been driven blank up to a plant-ation on a fellside. We used to practice it often. The birds have to be very carefully shepherded, however. Any at-tempt at forcing them may result in disaster. They simply rise and fly for the lower ground again.

It is not advisable to shoot coverts too often. Perhaps an interval of at least a fortnight should elapse between one shoot and another. Pheasants, even if they be semi-tame, may leave a covert altogether, if molested too often, and I know that the survivors of a shoot are always a degree wilder than they were before it. I have seen a thousand pheasants feeding on a ride the evening before a shoot. Next day about a quarter of them were shot, but the other three-quarters did not turn up the day after the battue. Even allowing a big margin for birds that had died from their wounds. I have never seen as many birds after a shoot as I would have expected to. The fact is that some get such a fright that they look for pastures new. So, it behoves one to allow a long quiet interval between each shoot.

On the day after a big pheasant shoot there is a pick-up of wounded and dead game. It is never as big as a grouse pick-up, but I once gathered twenty-six birds. That is exceptional, however. Pheasants are usually gathered fairly cleanly on the actual day of the shoot. Moreover, they do not have the grouse's habit of flying on for a quarter of a mile after being hit, then dropping stone dead; and the ground is barer.

I usually took my gun with me on pheasant pick-up days, and I have used it occasionally. Quite often I put a pheasant out of a hedgerow which could run but not fly. These I bagged, although I hated to fire at a bird within the covert. It was always my policy to keep the coverts as quiet as possible, so that the survivors might gain some confidence in human beings again.

Our tenant farmers used to get a couple of brace of pheasants after the first shoot. That is a wise gesture, I think. Besides being an act of courtesy, which is always wisdom, it made the farmers more tolerant of birds on their land, but not because they ever did any damage. The young pheasants were never far from the coverts until after the corn stooks were lifted, and they did no harm at seed-time, because they did not exist then. The generation of the previous year was practically gone, and that year's generation was not yet born. Sometimes I felt slightly sad when I thought how short was the average span of life of my pheasants. In the autumn the coverts were full of life. The pheasants were full-grown and in fine plumage. They fought with each other at feed times, and they fluttered noisily to their roosts at eventide. By springtime they were nearly all gone.

The technique of grouse driving differs somewhat from that of pheasant driving. There are usually fewer beaters for one thing, even if two lines are used ; and the beaters carry flags. For another thing, the guns need some sort of concealment, as the grouse can be a very wary bird. Then wind is a more important factor on an open moor than it is in the comparatively sheltered coverts. An unfavourable wind may alter the drives of a grouse shoot at the last minute. Again, on the moor there is no preliminary driving-in, as a rule. The beaters line-out, and drive the grouse on a tract of moor to the butts, which are placed to cut the natural line of flight of the birds. A line of flankers is run out from the end butts along the imaginary side of the drive to discourage birds from breaking to the right and left. Those flankers also carry flags, but they have to be extremely careful only to use them at the right time. Should they rise up and flag too hard at the wrong time, which is too soon, they may put the grouse back over the beaters.

There are all sorts of butts, from improvised stands behind stone walls, in peat-hags and gullies, to elaborate, stone-built structures with concrete floors. The latter kind are common on North Riding moors, where there is an abundance of suitable stone. I prefer to stand behind a wall, and if the grouse show a tendency to go slightly to one side, I move accordingly. There is one disadvantage in shooting from behind a wall. The grouse may be flying low to escape a head-on wind, and a front shot is, therefore, difficult, because the walls, in Yorkshire at any rate, are rather high. Then, when the grouse top the wall, they drop almost to ground-level straightaway, and that makes a tricky shot, but not a very satisfactory one either. The birds are flying comparatively slowly, and their flight is uncertain. I have seen those low birds missed consistently by men who could take a high grouse travelling with a strong wind without any trouble.

Although the lines of butts are chosen carefully to inter-cept the natural routes of the grouse, yet I know drives where the grouse go almost invariably to only one or two butts, unless, of course, a strong wind pushes them farther across to the others. That state of affairs is not always easy to remedy, because a row of butts usually serves two drives, one back and one forward, and if the butts were altered to suit the poor drive, the other one would suffer. Sometimes it is possible to extend the row of butts, however, and that gets over the difficulty. I know at least one place on the Swaledale moors where there are thirteen butts in the row. Some of the middle butts are common to each drive. The only difficulty with so many butts is the confusion in the minds of some of the guns as to where they ought to be. The guns used to move up two places after each drive, and the right-hand butt at the beginning of the day was number one.

That was the usual procedure, but at this particular row of butts the middle butt, that is, the seventh butt from either end, was number one. So long as there were seven guns in the party, and each member knew of this different method of counting, all was well, but if there were, say, eight guns in the party, and some of them did not know which was number one (and it had to be altered to cope with the extra gun) there was chaos. I once saw a mild row strike up be-tween two guns, who could not agree on their respective positions in the line. I never quite understood why that particular row of butts should have a different system of numbering, unless it was because most of the butts were not visible to each other. They were at the bottom of a shallow gill, and the middle butt was the only round one among them. It was, therefore, the most easily recognised one among the lot. That may have been the reason.

When I first went over to the moors, I was surprised that the butts were not permanently numbered with paint. That seemed to me then the best way to avoid misunderstandings, but I was told that permanently numbered butts caused

more confusion often than unnumbered butts, and I realised after maturer thought that that could easily be so. For
instance, if there were the same amount of butts in every
row as there were shooters in each party all would be plain
sailing ; but often a row of butts has an extra one or two
or even three added to an end to provide for an unfavourable wind. Say then that there are ten butts in a row
and six guns are shooting in them. Number one gun may
be in number one butt, or he might be, according to the
wind, in number five. Perhaps the return drive might
necessitate the occupation of the butts from number two
upwards, and if each gun moved up two places after every
drive, the painted number would simply be a nuisance,
because it would not correspond with the gun's number in
the line. It would, in fact, complicate a complication still
more.

The placing of guns at any shoot is usually quite fair.
The members draw their numbers out of a hat ; or some
other secret method is employed which ensures that there
is no favouritism. In consequence of that, unlucky good
shots may have to stand comparatively idle all day and
watch the luckier duds blaze away non-stop. A keeper does
not like to see that. If birds are going over the butts in
streams, he likes to see a good bag made, because it is on
the size of the bag that his reputation rests. That is a curious
fact. It matters not, although hundreds of birds have been
lost out of the drives by adverse winds, or although the
shooting has been desperately third-class, the question ever
after, when the day is discussed, will be : 'What was the
bag ?'

To be a good shot, I think that one ought to start shooting at a comparatively early age ; and to enjoy shooting
fully, one ought to be interested in more than the mere firing
of cartridges. The man who is bored unless he is standing
at the end of a drive shooting at clouds of birds like an
automaton is not a hundred per cent shooting man.

Gamekeeping to-day

The craft of gamekeeping is not so important today as it was, say, fifteen years ago ; and when I say gamekeeping, I mean the preservation of game alone. There are many men now engaged in the destruction of vermin, and those men may incidentally encourage game, but their primary function is to help agriculture. I am in that category.

The days when several men were kept on every big estate to rear pheasants and to superintend the shooting of them are past. It may be that those days will never return. Battues were the product of a leisurely age, an age when money was plentiful, and more important still, an age when money could buy almost everything. The war altered all that.

On the moors, perhaps, the keeper may continue to shine with a diminished light. He helps to populate a wilderness with grouse ; for those hardy birds can live and grow fat on the poorest ground if suitably encouraged. And although the contribution to the nation's larder from the shooting of grouse is comparatively small, yet every little helps. But there is one deadly enemy which may put the moorland keeper out of office. That enemy is grouse disease. It is a virulent scourge, and no cure for it has yet been devised. This year grouse seem to be fairly numerous, but during the last few years they almost suffered extinction in some places.

The effects of grouse disease must be seen to be believed. One season birds may be swarming ; pack after pack come over the guns until one might be forgiven for thinking that nothing could be more certain than the supply of grouse. In a good season grouse simply cannot be shot down on a first-class moor, but before another Twelfth dawns those legions can be almost completely wiped out by disease. I have seen that myself.

Like the scourges that affect humanity, grouse disease has its cycles. I think that poor food is the primary cause.

Grouse live mainly on heather; so it follows that their staple food must be good if it is to maintain health. Heather to the grouse is as milk to the child, or as rice is to the Japanese. Skim the milk and the child becomes rickety; polish the rice and the Japanese suffer from beri-beri.

Overcrowding also appears to have something to do with grouse disease, because it is always more virulent if the stock is too big after a shooting season; and I daresay that inbreeding is an even greater contributory cause. I know a moor where the bag of grouse can rise in six or seven years from two brace a day to five hundred brace a day. Even allowing for some immigration, most of the birds on that moor in a peak year must be related. When that happens, disease goes through the stock like wildfire. A regular changing of eggs from widely-separated moors would at least help to stop that evil. But on the whole the moorland keeper is in a better position than most of his kind.

The partridge keeper does have a certain amount of justification for his existence, because his charges are not considered to be so harmful to agriculture as pheasants. Nevertheless, he has an uphill job. He sees all sorts of pot-hunters roaming over his ground in pursuit of 'pests,' but those pests have many forms, and they are all edible. So the partridge keeper carries on, yet conscious that he is of little importance, unless, of course, he combines his job with the destruction of rabbits. In that case he may have to be at the beck and call of many who are not really his bosses, but he is at any rate happy in the knowledge that he is not entirely a luxury man.

But whatever ideas some people may have about the importance or otherwise of the gamekeeper in the scheme of national rehabilitation, there is no doubt in my mind that he is the conservator of wild life. While he is preserving his game birds and animals, he is at the same time helping other interesting creatures to survive. Song birds are assured of peace to rear their broods in a game preserve, which might be denied them in a 'sanctuary' for all wild life.

The actual job of gamekeeping is free from many of the inhibitions which oppress the ordinary working man. There are no set hours. The middle of the night is as good a time for doing a job as the middle of the day to a conscientious keeper. That freedom I have found attractive. When I had a large stock of pheasants under my charge, I often got up in the middle of the night to investigate a shot, and I have wandered around for hours, hoping that another would go off, so that I might locate the poacher. Or I have got np on wild, rainy nights to protect my birds from foxes.

I think that most men work better with a minimum of overseers. Even a fellow who doesn't care a great deal for work will peg away steadily if he knows that he is doing some good, and if he knows that he can start with something else when the job in hand palls. But the trend today is towards greater supervision and perhaps also towards mental inanition.

Miscellany

This is a section of odds and ends. The first item concerns the almost incredible acumen of rats. Usually I have no rats about the hut, but when one does appear, or rather, when one makes itself known by banging and scratching under the hut, I remove him at once either by means of poison or trap. On this particular occasion I was not present ; so the rat or rats had the freedom of the place.

When I went into Keswick Cottage Hospital for repairs, there were no signs of rats about the hut, nor had any rats been near it for months. On the day that I left for the hospital I put some packets of sugar on the shelf, which is six feet from the floor. It is fixed to the wall opposite the door, and is normally inaccessible to any animal. The packets of sugar were laid behind some books ; so one would have thought that the precious commodity was quite safe, even from any possible human being. So, I left the hut in a comparatively easy frame of mind.

A month and four days later I came back. Dr. Cameron was kind enough to drive me up to the gateway, and I carried my little suitcase up to the hut myself. When I opened the door the hut had the same appearance as when I left it, but a few minutes later, when I went out for coal, I noticed a hole in the floor just inside the doorway. It was obviously the work of rats. How they managed to chew a hole at that place is still a mystery to me, because the floor there is a good foot from the ground. Not until an hour or so later, however, did I discover that the rats had been at my sugar. They had chewed all the edges and corners of the packets, but luckily the contents had gone hard with the damp ; so no sugar had run out. To say that I was astonished is a mild summary of my feelings. I could not understand how the brutes had got on to the shelf, nor could I understand how they had been able to smell the sugar at that height. Then I noticed that a chair, a plain wooden chair at that, was quite near my Home Guard greatcoat, which was hanging from the shelf by a nail. The rats had got on to the chair and climbed up the inside of the greatcoat on to the shelf, then hopped over the books to the sugar. It was conclusive proof that rats are no fools. If I had been living in the hut, they would never have attempted such a thing ; but I should like to know how long they took to find out that the hut was unoccupied. They were clever, but they were not clever enough to leave alone the stuff that I dropped through the hole in the floor.

During the war I had a bit of bad luck with another scarce commodity, namely, plus-fours. Clothing coupons were none too plentiful ; so I rummaged out two old pairs of plus-fours, and decided that, if they were patched neatly by a tailor, they might give me a lot more service. An elderly artist, whom I often met on the road as I was going about my job, put me on to this thrifty scheme. He had practically resurrected several pairs of plus-fours by that method.

Accordingly, I took my two pairs of plus-fours to a

L

tailor in Keswick along with a lot of patching material. I
was told to call in three weeks for the repaired garments ;
so I was happy. Four weeks later (I allowed an extra week
for possible pressure of business) I decided to call for my
trousers ; but before I got there I happened to mention to
a farm man at Ullock that I was beating the clothes rationing
by having my plus-fours mended at a certain place. Then I
was told that the certain place had been burned out a
fortnight previously. That dampened my spirits somewhat.
When I got to the tailor's shop, I discovered that the bad
news was only too true. My two pairs of plus-fours had
gone up with a lot more things in smoke. The tailor offered
me two pounds as compensation, but I only took one. I saw
that the fellow was not too happy over the affair. He had
not been fully insured. Fate certainly brought off a long
shot that time.

Another vexatious incident was more of my own doing.
I had a couple of incubators in a shed behind the hut under
the big cherry tree. There was only one thermometer for the
two incubators, and it got broken ; so I biked over to the
Kennels for another. There were several at the Kennels ; so
I took the lot. One of them was a long thermometer for
testing the heat of the water in the tanks, and to save it from
injury I wrapped it along with the others in a piece of sacking, and put the package on my back. That seemed to be
the safest place for such fragile merchandise. Then I set off
for the hut. I gave my iron steed its head, and went down
by the side of Swinside Fell at a goodly pace. At the bend
at the bottom of Pow Howe brow I saw a piece of hedge-
clipping on the road in front of me, but whether my excessive speed or the clipping caused the disaster I do not
know. The clipping was stuck in the fork. In any case, I
turned a complete somersault, and landed flat on my back
in front of the bike, which was sadly battered. The thermometers were even more sadly battered. In fact, they were in
tiny splinters. Fortunately, I had no broken bones. I got the
bike on an even keel, but found that the front wheel would

not go round. It was buckled beyond redemption. The back
wheel was slightly out of true, but I stood on it and pulled
it at various points until I got it to function somehow. Then
I lifted up the fore-end, and pushed the bike in front of me
on one wheel. And that is how I brought the remains of the
thermometers to the hut.

The accident which I had down on the flooded Mire at
the head of Lake Bassenthwaite one chilly night in
January might have had a different ending.

My employer and I went there to flight ducks one Saturday evening. We waded through a flood to reach the lake
head, but when we reached our stance, the ground was,
rather strangely, comparatively dry. It was a dismal afternoon. Grey clouds rolled across the tops of the dark fells,
and the lake was choppy.

The ducks were not flighting that evening, probably
because there was a moon later, but we waited until the last
possible minute in the hope of a shot or two. Only two
ducks appeared the whole time that we stood at the lake
head. They went without a shot. One was lost in the blackness of Skiddaw ; the other came from behind. So, we set off
up the Mire in a gloom that was thickening rapidly.

When we came to the deepest part of the floodwater, I
had an idea that we were holding rather much to the left.
There was nothing, however, to guide me. Then quite
suddenly a thorn bush loomed in front of us. It seemed to
be one of the bushes that stand by the only bridge out of the
Mire, but we had reached it so quickly that I was confused.
I tucked my employer's shooting stick under my left arm-
pit, and groped for an electric torch, which I had in a
satchel. I shone it on the bush. It was a single bush where
several ought to have been. Moreover, between the bush
and me was a weed-covered expanse of floodwater. I took
two steps forward to investigate, and was immediately up
to the waist in icy water. My employer was a bit to my
right ; so he escaped.

I floundered deeper into the water, as I endeavoured to

turn, but I did manage to turn before I got up to the neck. Only a thick mat of weeds prevented that. Finally, I grasped a tuft of rushes with my left hand and, with some difficulty, I hauled myself out of the water. Unwittingly, I had stumbled into the boundary ditch. It and the floodwater were one. I kept hold of my torch the whole time, although it was under water for several seconds, but the shooting stick dropped when I grasped the rushes. It has never been seen to this day.

I did go down with a boathook on the Monday after the mishap, but it was useless, although it was about seven feet long. A few days later I got a nine foot drag from some Catchment Board men, and it was none too long. I had it into the ditch right to the hilt, but the shooting stick remains yet in the mud. Probably I trampled it in as I struggled to get out.

Some years ago an old, retired farmer was drowned in that same ditch. He had apparently spent his youth in this district, but his later life had been spent somewhere in West Cumberland. As far as I could gather at the time, he got off a bus at Braithwaite one winter evening as dusk was falling. A fowler saw him making towards the Bog, and that was the last time that anyone saw him alive. A hue and cry for him got up a few days later, and the Bog was scoured by the police and a company of searchers. After a lot of trouble they found him drowned in the treacherous sump, where I had my mishap. The part of the Bog nearest to the lake is, by the way, usually called the Mire, probably because it is a real mire in many places. It surprises me even now that the poor man ever got on to the Mire. There are many places on the way there where a feeble, old man could easily have drowned. The Bog is a risky place to those who know it thoroughly, but it is a veritable death trap to any comparative stranger at night.

A tinker woman also got her end there one black night many years ago, but I think that she died of exposure. No doubt, she realised that she had got into a dangerous place, and had lain down to wait for daylight. When daylight came wanly over Skiddaw, she had found a greater peace than she had ever known in life.

Talking of lost people reminds me of Billy Landels, a keeper who used to be here. Billy went fox-hunting one winter day on the fells between Newlands Valley and Borrowdale, and towards mid-afternoon a thick mist descended on the tops. He decided to make for the Kennels via Maiden Moor, Yewthwaite Coomb, and Catbells. For a long time he walked, and a lift in the mist enabled him to see around him a bit. To his astonishment he found that he was looking down on the village of Rosthwaite in Borrowdale. He was, in fact, almost at his starting place, and had quite obviously walked in a circle. I had heard of such happenings, but I never knew anyone personally until then who had had the experience of walking in a circle in a mist without being aware that he was doing so.

Billy was a good walker. He and I set off one Sunday morning for a longer hike than I would care to undertake nowadays. It was March or April. The morning was just right for walking, neither too hot nor too cold. We set off up Whinlatter Pass from Braithwaite, and reached Lorton Village some time before midday. Billy elected to quench his thirst at the White Horse Inn ; so we entered the pub and ordered drinks. Billy had a pint of beer, but I contented myself with lemonade. The beer was apparently like cream. Billy said so, anyway, and he would have stopped to sample it further, but I persuaded him to move at the end of that one pint. It is a glorious walk up by Crummock Water to Buttermere. That introduction to another facet of Lakeland beauty remains with me yet as a rare experience. I loved the vista of blue fells around Buttermere, and when we were approaching Honister Pass, I drew out my sketch book, and made a quick note of the rugged lines of the fells and of the placid lake that lies entrancingly beneath. Billy waited while I drew my sketch, but I suspect that he was quite pleased when I put the book back into my pocket. Billy did not devote much time to artistic affairs.

Honister Crag inpressed me immensely. It still impresses me. That stupendous wall of rock is the sheerest crag that I have ever seen.

At the top of the Pass we met an aquaintance, who worked in the slate quarries that honeycomb the Crag. He was slightly tipsy, and insisted in telling us a rigmarole about a keeper who used to be here. The keeper had apparently been watching him while he was looking some snares up Newlands Valley, and the tipsy one had threatened to shoot his legs off. The story might have gone down better with us, if we had not known him pretty thoroughly.

We had tea that afternoon at Rosthwaite in Borrowdale, and we were quite ready for it. I don't think that we had anything to eat between then and breakfast-time. Then we set off down through the Jaws of Borrowdale as dusk was falling. It was completely dark when we arrived at the Kennels. It was chilly also, but Billy soon had a roaring fire going in the bothy, and we sat down to a real feed. I remember that as the fitting end to a wonderful day.

One lovely summer evening a friend and I biked a good part of that same route, but we went in the opposite direction. We went up the valley and over Newlands Hause, instead of taking the Borrowdale road. The ride down to Buttermere in the golden light of sunset was a dream, and I loved the pearly light that softened the fells as we biked by Crummock Water hardly less. Dusk was falling as we climbed Whinlatter Pass, but twilight is long in midsummer; so we arrived at Braithwaite before the shadows had entirely closed in. The roads that wind through the valleys that bound the Derwent Fells will always be lovely to me, and they will always be lovely to those who look with the seeing eye. If there is a more beautiful route on earth, it must indeed be beautiful.

This Lakeland can be cruel, however, to those who seek her fastnesses. Every year that I can remember someone has paid the penalty for taking those serene-looking fells too casually. The latest mountain fatality occurred in Whelpside Ghyll on Helvellyn. Two young Manchester men met their ends there in a fearful blizzard. That day, Easter Saturday, was bad enough here in the valley. What it was like on the bleak, snow-covered fellside I shudder to think. The weather was so bad that I hesitated to go to Keswick for my usual rations. According to the Press report, those two young men left Patterdale Youths' Hostel to climb over the tops to Honister. They were never seen alive again. A Corporation worker, who is employed at Thirlmere Waterworks, found one of them lying in a pool, when he was searching for lost sheep. Shortly after, the other body was found by one of his mates. A Keswick doctor certified that the last-found one had died from multiple injuries. He had a broken left thigh and two fractured bones in the left forearm. It was assumed that these injuries had rendered him so helpless that his mate had arranged some clothing over him (the doctor said that he could not have done that himself) and gone to seek help. On the way down, the deep snow in the ghyll had betrayed his footing, and he had plunged to his death in the pool. Probably he had been knocked unconscious before he got into the water, but drowning was certified as the cause of his death. If there had been no snow on Helvellyn, it would still not have been a suitable day for negotiating that rocky, exposed terrain. It was remarkable, nevertheless, that both should have died.

I remember a tragedy of another sort that occurred many years ago at the Jaws of Borrowdale. It was foul play that time. A Chinese lady was found in Cumma Catta Wood, dead. She had been strangled with a piece of window cord. One of the first persons on the scene was, rather unluckily for the murderer, a detective on holiday from, I think, Liverpool. When the hue and cry got up, it was discovered that a Chinese couple had been lodging at a nearby boarding-house. On the day of the murder the husband came back alone, and said that his wife had gone off to Keswick to buy stockings. However, the police, investigating quietly, found that some cord had been removed from a window in the room where the Chinese couple had had their quarters. The husband was arrested, and was eventually hanged. As far as I can remember, he said in his defence that he had merely been the instrument of some Chinese secret society. Whether he was that or not I never discovered, but he took an extremely clumsy way of fulfilling his obligations if it were so.

When I see Billy Wren, one of the roadmen, I am reminded of a tragedy of yet another kind which occurred on the Borrowdale side of Honister Pass. Billy walks somewhat splay-footed, but he is fortunate to be able to walk at all. He has told me more than once that his foot was looking in the opposite direction, when he recovered consciousness. The accident was the result of a waggon, full of County Council workers, running away on that fearfully steep gradient. Apparently, the driver was unable to change into low gear, and his brakes would not take any effect ; so the waggon whizzed on until it overturned. Some men were killed, and a lot more were injured. I should imagine that the vehicle went like an express train before it crashed. For months Billy's foot was in danger. A bone was removed, and finally he was able to hobble out, but even today he feels sometimes that it is not nearly such a good member as the other.

But enough of tragedies. Let us devote a short paragraph to Swinside Inn, commonly called Swinside Jerry, which is the dalesman's focal point in this valley. It was built, I daresay, many hundreds of years ago, and until recently it looked its age. Just before the war it was remodelled ; so its antiquity is not so apparent. Moreover, it has extended its scope. One can get a snack or a tea there nowadays. Formerly, it was purely and simply an alehouse.

During the war it was a favourite rendezvous with the soldiers and ATS girls who were stationed near Keswick.

On Sunday evenings, particularly in the summer, one could hear some good musical talent in the side room. I have listened to impromptu concerts from the vantage point of the gateway into Sim Thwaite's field opposite, and I was delighted often with the quality of the singing and the playing. Personally I did not attend, because I practically drink nothing stronger than lemonade.

In the earlier days when Swinside Inn was a picturesques old, bulging-walled, sagging-roofed structure, the habitues were nearly always dalesmen. There were regular attender, who seldom missed a night. In the winter evenings they sat round the fire, and retailed stories of fox-hunting, lead-mining, farming and poaching, until the old lady, who had it then, turned them out into the blustery darkness. Those regular customers were characters. They swallowed a good many pints each evening, and on gala nights they had a few more to celebrate. One old warrior claimed that he drank twenty-five pints before he lost count. He certainly had a capacity for beer, but whether any human being could drink twenty-five pints in one evening is a matter for debate.

That old fellow worked on the estate, and he never possessed a watch. That was no great handicap usually, because he could get the time from his workmates. One time, however, he had to work alone in one of those plantations on Swinside Fell ; so he solved the no-watch problem by taking the alarm clock up to the plantation with him. It stopped there under a big spruce tree in a biscuit tin. A keeper came past one day, and was astonished to hear a ticking in the box. 'I thought it was some sort of infernal machine,' he confided to me. It would have certainly been an 'alarming' find in other circumstances. Please excuse the pun.

But that old chap is gone now. I thought that he was so tough that he would live to be a hundred, but he became crippled with rheumatism, and died peacefully. He did not do so badly. I believe his age when he died was seventy-eight. When he retired from the estate, he employed a lot of his leisure in cutting whins and carrying them home on a trolley for firewood.

Another old dalesman who is now gone, and who was a regular attender at the Inn, had a great capacity for pawky anecdote. He was a fairly skilled mason, although I do not think that he ever served his apprenticeship to that trade. Normally he was hired on some of the dale farms. Once he was asked by a farmer's wife (so the story goes) to take out the oven, and re-build the flues, so that they might draw better. All this had to be done while the farmer's wife was away at Keswick on a shopping expedition one Saturday forenoon. The amateur mason did the job, and when the lady returned, the oven was back in its position, and everything was spick and span. Moreover, the fire was lit, but the damper was not drawn. The lady went to the fireplace, and was about to draw the damper to see how the new arrangement worked, when the hired man spoke up in alarm. 'Tak' care, Missus!' he said. 'When Ah pulled damper afore ta test it, t'cat was lyin' asleep on t'hearth-rug an' afore Ah could catch hold on it, it hed vanished up t'chimla.' The flues had undoubtedly been improved in the lady's absence!

At one time the Blencathra fox-hounds put up at Swinside Inn, when they were hunting the fells above Newlands Valley. They usually stopped a week, and it was a busy week at the old place. The hunters gathered there after a kill to discuss every aspect of the chase. They also drank a considerable quantity of beer. It was a picturesque sight when the scarlet-coated huntsman left the Inn on a calm autumn morning with the hounds on their couples. Sometimes there was a 'lowse' on Swinside Fell behind the Inn, and a fox was generally found either among the bracken or in the crag face, but it was seldom that the fox stopped on Swinside Fell. Off he would go across the valley to Barrow, with the pack in full cry. One would see the hounds go up Barrow face in a sinuous line, then the hunt would disappear over the shoulder into Smeltmill Ghyll. As far as I was concerned, that was the end of the hunt, but enthusiasts followed up hill and down dale, until they finally landed at Buttermere or Crummock Water. Fell hunting is a strenuous exercise.

The view from Swinside Inn is extremely fine. There are fells everywhere around. Straight across the valley is Causey Pike, which is one of my favourite mountains. I like its symmetrical cone formation. Down the valley one can see the deep blue of Barf. When the sun shines, all the fells are lovely. I used to think that Borrowdale was very attractive, and I still love its seclusion, but on the whole, I feel that Newlands Valley is incomparable.

Across the valley from the Inn is a whitewashed cottage, which used to house a keeper. Occasionally he went to the Jerry, as it is called, for a glass of beer and a talk with the regular attenders. One winter night he got a little more than usual, and was not too sure of his feet as ten o'clock was approaching. However, he decided to go home before closing time. Some of his pals offered to see him safely over the beck bridge, which had then no parapets, but he would not hear of assistance. Off he went into the darkness. The ones who were left were worried ; so a dalesman got up and followed him at a discreet distance. If the keeper did fall into the beck, someone would be at hand to pull him out. He got over the bridge safely, however, and went to bed quite unconscious that he had been followed ; but the Good Samaritan was not so lucky. He fell into the beck ! Evidently the Good Samaritan was even more befogged with beer than the keeper.

On the roadway that runs down from Swinside Inn, that is, by the foot of Swinside Fell, I have often seen hag worms, or blind worms, as they are commonly called, basking in the sunlight of a summer's morning. I have only once seen a hag worm elsewhere. That was by the side of this wood. For some reason, unknown to me, those snake-like creatures prefer the far side of the valley. Often they are cut to pieces by cars, and often they are killed by ignorant people for adders. I see their remains as I travel to and fro between the hut and the Kennels. They seem to be more plentiful some years than others. This year, despite the hot spell, I have not seen one. I wonder whether the long time of snow and ice which we had at the beginning of spring has anything to do with their unusual scarcity.

Speaking of worms reminds me that I have only once seen a glow-worm in the Lake District, or anywhere else, for that matter. It was on a grass verge by the side of a wood near Derwentwater that I saw it one summer night. I picked it up, and put it in a big jar among some grass, fully expecting that it would emit light indefinitely, but I was disappointed. The light went after a day or so.

As for lizards, active relations of the hag worms, I have also only seen one here. That happened on the side of Barrow that looks into Smeltmill Ghyll. One lovely morning I climbed up the face of Barrow to see a buzzard's nest, which was being prepared in a crag that overlooks Newlands Valley. I was too early to see any eggs, but a fresh platform of green larch twigs had been added to the nest of the previous year. It was so beautiful on the fell side that I walked round into Smeltmill Ghyll on a sheep-track, and it was on the sheep-track that I saw the lizard. It scuttled away in front of me very rapidly indeed, and vanished into the longish heather. I was glad that I had seen the unusual creature. The keepers in Swaledale tell me that lizards are common on the moors. They live in the peat-hags, apparently. Why they should be so rare here I do not know.

When I went back to look at that buzzard's nest, I found that it had been robbed. That sort of thing happens with annoying frequency. Last year on Swinside Fell the same tale was told. A pair of buzzards had their nest in a Scots fir tree just below the highest plantation. Some boys found it, and took the eggs. The Sunday after the robbery I caught some boys on the fell after further plunder. They gave me the names of the buzzard nest despoilers, but as they were not easily accessible, I contented myself with warning the informers, and bidding them pass on the warning to the others. Since then I have never met those boys where they ought not to be. Nevertheless, there are many more at the same senseless game. It is a well-hidden nest, indeed, that escapes everybody's eyes.

My helper in the rearing-field and I once saw a buzzard try to catch a small bird, which seemed to us to be chaffinch. Our rearing-field was at the foot of Rowling-End Fell. One sunny morning after breakfast we were having a chat before we started with the mid-morning feed, when we noticed the buzzard doing a lot of foolish acrobatics on the front of Ellas Crag, which was only about a hundred yards over the fell wall. It must have conceived a dislike to the chaffinch, because I have never known a buzzard bother with such small prey. It had not the slightest chance of catching the little bird. The chaffinch, to use an ordinary expression, made rings round it. We laughed to see the great hawk turning somersaults in the air and always striking where the chaffinch was not. Finally, it gave up the attempt, and soared away into the blueness.

Buzzards are usually content with rabbits and even carrion. They are not so faddy as some hawks are. We were never bothered much with them among the hand-reared pheasants, but when one did start, it could be almost as crafty as a sparrowhawk, and it could kill big pheasant poults. The buzzard's usual method of killing pheasants was to sit on a tree until a chance presented itself, then swoop down on the unfortunate pheasant. On one or two occasions I have known buzzards hover like a kestrel and swoop down on pheasants with closed wings. Only on one occasion have I seen a buzzard lift a tiny pheasant chick from the rearing-field. That occurred up the valley near Yewthwaite old lead mine.

That season when we reared pheasants in the fields at the foot of Rowling-End Fell, we were bothered a lot by jackdaws. Those artful creatures killed a goodly few birds, but they never to my knowledge carried them away. I think

M

that the jackdaws were merely after the pheasant feed, and killed the chicks out of jealousy. They used to nest in Ellas Crag in hordes, and also in Ullock Crag on Swinside Fell, and on the slaty, dangerous face of Barf below Thornthwaite. Now there is never a jackdaw nest in those crags. Boys, at the veritable risk of their lives, have harried them until they dare not try to rear a family in any of those places. I think that the crags above Lodore on the road to Borrowdale is the favoured nesting-site nowadays. This spring they were wheeling about there in hundreds.

Beside a certain few coops near the fell wall in one of those Rowling-End rearing-fields I noticed stones lying one day, which I had no recollection of having seen when I put the coops there first. The stones increased; so I paid particular attention to that place, although it was not easily seen from the feeding hut. The wall bent slightly towards Smeltmill Ghyll there. Then I discovered how the stones had arrived. A little boy from a nearby farm, who attended Newlands school, came along the road behind the wall on his way home every afternoon, and he stopped opposite those coops to pelt stones at the pheasant chicks. I don't think he had ever managed to hit one, because I never missed a bird, nor did I see any lame ones, but the boy evidently tried hard to register a hit. The stones were mute testimony to that. I gave him some trenchant advice, and no more stones fell into the rearing-field.

Near those same coops grew some briar-rose bushes. One evening I found a chaffinch caught by a wing on a thorn in one of them. The wing was practically shattered by the poor bird's struggles to get free. I had never known of such a happening before, nor have I ever known of anything similar since, excepting perhaps a rabbit which caught itself by a hind leg in a wire-netting fence, which had a strand of plain wire running through it. The leg was securely fixed between the wire of the mesh and the single, plain wire. When I say that I have never known anything similar, I mean among wild creatures. They are usually too wide-awake to be caught accidentally, but sheep and dogs are often hitched up on fences between the two top wires.

Over there on Swinside Fell I once found two sheep hanging dead from the forks of laurel bushes that grow above the plantation. They had been reaching up to get at the foliage, and as they dropped back, they had each caught a foreleg firmly in a fork. Their own weight and their struggles to get free did the rest. Thus they perished miserably. It was perhaps rather remarkable that two should have caught themselves so near together. They were only about twenty-five yards apart, and they are the only two sheep that I have seen caught in such a manner in my life.

As I roam about the countryside, I occasionally see freaks of wild life. A year or two ago I saw a crow, which seemed to be a carrion, in the meadows up the beckside, and it had white wings. It was a curious-looking object among the others. Then I saw another crow more recently with white feathers in the middle of its tail. I have seen piebald blackbirds also, and twice I have seen a white robin. At least, I assumed they were robins from their shape and movements. One spent a winter below the hut. The other I only saw twice. It was sitting on a gatepost at Swinside Lodge boarding-house one morning when I went past on my way to the Kennels to feed my ferrets. I saw it fly into some rhododendron bushes just after I passed the gateway. On my way back I overtook the headmaster of the boys' school at Hawse-End, and I told him of the freak, but I did not expect that we should see it. To my surprise, it was sitting on the gatepost where I had seen it on my way in. Never have I seen it again. That morning a kestrel was gliding about the meadows between Swinside Lodge and the Moss nearby ; so there may have been a tragedy. Such an odd creature would attract unwelcome attention, I daresay.

Almost every season in the rearing-fields there are albino, or part-albino pheasants. Usually they die before a month is up, but if they can survive the month, they may grow up to be good birds. The pure albinos are the more weakly ones.

Other freaks had more than their quota of legs. One that I remember particularly had an extra leg growing from its rump. It grew up, however, and the odd leg shrivelled away. When it left the rearing field, it was as good as the others.

Occasionally a bird is neither a cock nor a hen, but any hermaphrodite pheasant that I have seen was more of a hen than a cock. Those freaks appear to be quite healthy and vigorous. When they are shot they are as plump as the normal ones.

The most common freakish feature among rabbits is a malformation of the teeth. Whether it is the result of injury, or it is some inherited trait I do not know. It can be the result of both, I suppose, but in any case, the rabbit dies eventually of starvation. The teeth apparently do not meet properly, and cannot, therefore, be kept ground down ; so they grow and grow until they are like miniature elephants' tusks. By that time, of course, the poor creature is a bag of bones.

This year I have seen several black rabbits. They are not, as one might suppose, the offspring of a tame rabbit that has got its liberty. They are freaks. Last year there were rabbits with white fore quarters. They were also freaks. No doubt, all the variety of Nature is the result of freaks.

Now, here is a question that has caused a lot of discussion among naturalists and shooting men and gamekeepers and all those who are interested in wild life : Does the woodcock carry its young ? A lot of apparently reliable watchers have claimed that the woodcock does carry its young, but I might as well say that I am extremely doubtful. I have seen woodcocks many a time go through the motions of carrying their young when suddenly disturbed by me, but I have not proved to my satisfaction that any young one was actually carried ; but I have proved that a woodcock which appeared to be carrying a young one could not possibly have been carrying one of her own brood, and that was simply because the individuals of the brood were almost as big as herself. Moreover, they could all fly almost as well as the parent, and had, therefore, no need to be carried. That instance, which I remember so clearly, occurred at Swinside Moss.

I disturbed the woodcock family there one day in August, yes, in August. The mother flew off in great distress. She uttered the pitiful cries that all woodcocks utter in similar circumstances, and she had great difficulty in flying. As she dodged among the trees, one might have been forgiven for imagining that she carried one of her young. About fifty yards away she settled, still calling pitifully ; so I went towards her, knowing perfectly well that she was trying to lure me away from where I was standing, because the young were crouching near. As I approached her, she took to wing with the customary woodcock agility, and went farther down the wood. I notice that the woodcock always ceases to 'carry her young' when she gets the human being safely away from where the brood is squatting.

On that particular day I went back to where I rose the old woodcock, and I searched carefully among the scanty, stunted bracken that was growing among the trees. Four young woodcock flew away, one after another. I took careful note that they were nearly as big as the parent bird. They did not require carrying, and I doubt whether the old bird could have lifted any one of them clear of the ground, even if she had been equipped with talons.

I have seen scores of woodcock with their young. The wood on the north shore of Derwentwater used to hold many broods every year. They bred early and late. I have even seen young woodcocks in August that could not fly, but only once. Most of the young woodcocks appeared in the late spring. I have, therefore, had ample opportunities for noting the antics of old woodcocks when they are rearing their young, and the description which I have already given will fit almost every case.

One amateur naturalist said to me recently that the woodcock was not supposed solely to lift a young one when disturbed by human beings, but that she carried them one by one in the evenings to the feeding grounds. Then I will say emphatically that I have never seen a woodcock carry anything at all during the evening flight to the bird's feeding grounds.

A writer in a weekly journal made me suspect his powers of observation, when he stated that the woodcock carried her young tucked under one wing. No bird could fly at all with a chick under one wing. I think that I am right when I say that, because we used to pinion our hen pheasants on one wing, and that kept them very effectively from flying out of their laying pens. If both wings had been pinioned, it might have been possible for a bird to fly slightly, because the balance would have been better, but even then, the flight could only have been short. I have, in fact, known of birds with both wings clipped that were able to get out of a fairly high pen by taking advantage of bushes, but no bird, to my knowledge, ever got out of a pen if it had only one wing clipped, except through a hole in the netting. So I conclude that the 'observer' who saw a woodcock carry a chick under one wing wasn't too reliable.

However, the old controversy will go on. Someone will always be found who has seen the woodcock carry her young somehow or other, but I feel now after years of first-hand knowledge that I shall never see that interesting ornithological phenomenon. And on that note I will end the section of odds and ends.

Living in a Hut

It is remarkable how many people yearn to return to a more primitive, more simple way of living. That is proved by the amount of caravans and trailers that are drawn into fields and lanes everywhere, but particularly in the Lake District, during summer. The owners of those caravans and trailers can only be amateur Bohemians. They are caught inexorably in the net of our pseudo-civilization, and they must abide by its rules, even although they do pretend that they have cast those rules aside for a few weeks each year.

Living the simple life alone has, however, its penalties as well as its rewards. I, for instance, have to do every single little chore myself. If my dishes are not washed up when I leave in the morning, they are still unwashed when I return, be it midday or evening. If I fail to bring in fire-wood, and find that I am hindered thereby in the morning, I have nobody to blame but myself. If I come home cold and hungry some winter evening and the fire is out, I have to set to work to get the fire going and to prepare myself a meal. I cannot sit down, draw on my slippers, and wait for something hot and tasty to appear.

So the person who would live successfully in a hut must cultivate some sort of routine, and there are several essential jobs that one must invariably attend to. For instance, I always fill up the kettle, even if I only take a cupful out of it. I always go to the spring for water, when the bucket is empty or nearly empty, even if it is somewhat inconvenient to do so. Again : I contrive to have a supply of kindling wood drying in the oven, in case I come back and find the fire out, although I always bank up the fire when I leave the hut, and it is, therefore, generally alight when I return. In the cupboard I try to have a small stock of food in hand. On a line below the mantelpiece I have dry stockings hanging, so that I can change with the minimum of delay, if I come in with wet feet. Should I come in wet through, I hang my clothes in front of the fire at once, and they are ready again when I need them. Those are only a few of my routine items. They may not seem to be important, but failure to attend to any of them results in muddle and vexation for me.

Now and then, I have forgotten some of those duties. I have left an empty water bucket. Then I have returned in a lashing rain-storm at dusk, and found that I had to struggle along the wood to the spring, when I could have been sitting comfortably by the fire. Or I have wakened some rainy morning and found that I had no kindling wood in the oven. Vexation and hindrance ! It is a fact that experience is the best teacher. Punishment follows neglect immediately.

One of the rewards of living alone in a hut in a beautiful district is peace, peace to meditate, peace to contrive things, and peace from the empty shams and insincerities of present human society. But make no mistake. I like people, usually. I am probably more indulgent towards the frailnesses of humans than many people are, and it gives me little pleasure to discuss the shortcomings of my fellow men. On the other hand, I am generally aware of the fact when anyone is trying to 'do' me.

Sometimes I have been asked point blank why I live in a hut. My answer is that I like to live in a hut ; but that is much too simple an explanation for some people. They think that there must be one definite reason for such eccentric behaviour, some episode in the dim past, and I can hardly convince them otherwise. A psychologist might give a reason, but I assure anyone that no one reason can be found that made me live in a hut. Chance had a lot to do with it really. I could just as easily have been living in a Council house today in a busy street, or in the backwoods of Canada. It was an advert. in two Scottish papers that took me here, and Fate provided the hut. It has stood the years well, and I hope that it will continue to withstand them.

One must have a certain amount of good health to live successfully in a hut, however. The man who is always ailing is asking for trouble, if he lives alone. He could be with the angels for days, and no one would be any the wiser, until some curious person came to see why the chimney was not smoking. That is the great drawback of living alone. When illness comes, the most independent hut-dweller finds that he needs the rest of the human race after all.

The fact remains that a great many people wish to get back to a freer, more primitive way of living. Civilization palls often. People find that others dominate their lives too much. They have to study this one and that one before they can move. They cease to express themselves, and they fritter away their days full of vague frustrations.

Piping

During all those years that I have lived in the hut, I have retained an enthusiasm for the bagpipes. Not every night, but several times a week, I throw the drones over my left shoulder and play a few marches, strathspeys and reels.

I prefer marches, because they have more feeling in them than the dance tunes, but I seldom play Pibroch, the classical music, although it is all feeling. I like something tuneful, and moreover, an English audience (and many a Scottish one also) would certainly say that I was a poor player if they heard the solemn repetitions of the Great Music. To play Pibroch (or Piobaireachd, to give it its Gaelic name) one's pipes must be of the finest make. Any sharpness or flatness in the chanter is fatal to the true expression of Ceol Mor.

Often I play outside the hut ; so my audience is somewhat scattered. People at Keswick have heard the pipes. That's two and a half miles away, but only on the calmest of summer evenings is it possible to hear my playing at that distance.

People have evolved all sorts of theories to account for my outdoor playing. Some said that I was scaring foxes, when these woods were full of pheasants, but nobody, as far as I know, ever accused me of trying to entice foxes as the Pied Piper enticed rats. Actually, a piper hears his music better in an unenclosed place, although a big room where the acoustics are good does as well. This hut, I'm afraid, gives a foggy echo to the voice of even a first-class set of pipes.

About twelve years ago I decided that playing the pipes was not enough. I felt that I ought to compose something. Other pipers had composed the tunes which I had enjoyed so often ; therefore, I owed something for that pleasure. One day I sat down with a pencil and a blank manuscript book, and the result was a semi-pibroch which I named 'Inverbervie Gathering.' Since then I have filled one thick, well-bound manuscript book and several smaller, paper-backed ones with pipe compositions. The total amount of original tunes in the thick book is two hundred and fourteen. The others I haven't counted, but I estimate that I have composed about two hundred and fifty pipe tunes.

Another bagpipe enthusiast in the district was Sandy Coutts, the river watcher. I say 'was,' because Sandy has practically retired from piping, although he still lives here. During the war he instructed an R.A.F. pipe band, and the non-stop piping got on to his nerves so badly that he sold his own instrument. Now he gets most of his music out of a wireless set.

When Sandy came to the Lake District, he lived in a hut on the edge of Derwent Bog. Many a good night with the pipes have I had there. Often as I approached the little building in the darkness, I have heard the shrill music from afar. At first I would hear it faintly, then as I got nearer, the booming of the drones would become audible, and when I opened the door, there would be a veritable cataract of grace-notes. Sandy would be parading the floor, blowing all he was able to, oblivious to everything except his music. That's how the pipes affect one. Nowadays Sandy lives respectably in a stone house like most other people. No more Bohemian nights for him.

Seton Gordon, the naturalist and piper, came one night to visit me. He had been climbing and walking in the Lake District for a few days, and in his travels had met the village schoolmaster, who told him that I was also a piper; so Seton Gordon, accompanied by the village schoolmaster and a local retired gentleman, arrived at the hut. I was preparing for an all-night session with the Home Guard, and my time was therefore limited, but we had a good ceilidh, as the Gaelic-speakers say.

My piping visitor favoured the classical music. Even now, the memory of that evening comes vividly to me. I see Seton Gordon, a tall figure in the kilt, pacing the hut floor over by that chest of drawers. The other two visitors are seated by the fire, but I stand at the bedroom doorway. The light is not very brilliant (I had not my Tilley lamp then) but it gleams on the silver mountings of the pipes and on the haft of the dirk in the piper's stocking top. When the pibroch finishes, I lift my pipes and play a few regimental marches. At nine-thirty my visitors depart reluctantly.

I am somewhat ashamed to admit that before the visit I did not know Seton Gordon's reputation as a naturalist. Since then I have seen and admired his bird photographs and nature writings. Actually, I had seen the name, but did realise that at the time. In the spate of literature which pours from the presses nowadays individual names are apt to become submerged. When the naturalist-piper got back to his home in the Isle of Skye, he wrote an article for *The Scotsman*, describing his Lakeland tour. At the end of it was a description of our ceilidh in this hut. I still have the newspaper cutting.

But pipers are not common in Cumberland. Many years ago, however, I did meet one near Swinside Cottages. He was Jock Stuart from Dunkeld, at one time well-known at Highland Gatherings, but then travelling the roads. He was a first-class piper, despite his lack of glamour. Jock told me that I would find a tune of his composition in the Cowal book of pipe music. It was there sure enough. Its title is 'Angus Macrae's Farewell to Blair Castle.' The notation could perhaps be altered to modern standards, but the tune was deemed worthy of a place in the book by competent judges.

The only other itinerant piper I have met here caused

a slight misunderstanding. He arrived at the village one Saturday evening, dressed in full regimentals, but with a down-at-heel aspect, asking for me. I learned later that he used my first name as if we were old pals.

Tyson Bragg, who had a shop in the village then, was trying to direct him to the hut when Jock Lowe, a friend of mine, passed ; so Jock volunteered to act as guide.

The pair arrived at the hut door in the gloaming. I asked them to step inside, thinking that Jock had brought some piping relation or acquaintance for a talk on the old instrument. So we were both under a misapprehension. Jock thought that the kiltie was a relation of mine !

Jock stood by the fireplace while the piper sat and talked to me about the various places in which he had played. Still it did not dawn on me that he had been playing in the streets. I thought he had been at social functions, or at competitions.

As time went on, Jock grew more and more mystified, and I grew more and more mystified. To Jock he appeared to be less and less a relation of mine, and to me he appeared to be less and less a relation of Jock. But at length the voluble piper disclosed the object of his visit. He wanted a pipe chanter reed. Some innkeeper in Keswick had recommended me as the only person in the district who might be able to supply his want. When I heard that, I hastened to get a reed for him, although I was by no means well-off for reeds at the time.

While I was getting the article, the piper picked up my practice chanter, which was lying on the table, and regaled us with a selection of pipe melodies. Obviously he was no McCrimmon!

When he got the reed, he looked at it for a few seconds with his head to one side, and remarked that it was 'a gey shorrrrt yin.' I agreed that it was a gey shorrrrt yin, but I did not say it was short because I had cut a bit off it. The reed had originally been too weak, and when I cut a bit off it, it became too strong. I suggested that he steep it in water overnight, but he had a better idea. He put it in his mouth, and kept it there until he reached the Royal Oak Inn barn, where he spent the night.

Next morning Jock considerately provided him with a feed, and he departed. Only in one way did he resemble McCrimmon of the famous Piobaireachd. He did not return.

Epilogue

This is the end of my book. I cannot say very definitely why I had such an insistent urge to write it, but write it I had to. Perhaps I realised that I could not live forever in a hut, and I wished to record some of the experiences and observations which have come to me during the years I have lived here. This is a free, almost Bohemian life. I have a certain job to do, and so long as I do it efficiently, I can come and go as I please. I can return from the Bog, wet to the knees, and nobody greets me with a long face, and I can put my feet up on the oven door and read in peace on a winter night without having to consult anyone but myself. As the shadows of life lengthen, however, that freedom may lose some of its glamour. I have had occasion to suspect that. One Saturday afternoon I went to a funeral at Crosthwaite Churchyard. It was a raw, bitter day. About four o'clock I got back to the hut, and went almost immediately to bed. As the evening advanced, I felt worse. 'Flu was rampant at the time and I felt that I had caught a dose. Nor was I wrong. I couldn't keep warm, although all the blankets I possessed were piled above me, and on the top of those was my Home Guard greatcoat. All night I was semi-delirious. I was neither asleep nor awake, and my head ached intolerably. One good act I performed before I went to bed was to stoke up the fire. Luckily, I had plenty of coal, and I needed it. There was a searing frost that night.

When Sunday dawned, I was no better. I drank some blackcurrant tea, but merely as a duty. I had no desire for anything. Then I stoked up the fire afresh, brought in some more coal, and went to bed again. No one called on Sunday. It was a day of ferocious cold. I lay with a splitting headache, and watched the daylight fade once more. There were long hours of darkness after that, then Monday dawned. Still I lay with a tumbled mass of blankets and a greatcoat on me. Thus Monday passed, and the early night came. I began to wonder whether I was having pneumonia, and I felt vaguely alarmed.

I had eaten nothing at all since Saturday, but on Tuesday morning I felt somewhat better, though far from right ; so I decided to get up and eat something, even although I didn't particularly want to. In the afternoon I had to deliver four rabbits at the Big House. Luckily, I had them at hand. They had been hanging on a fir tree near the hut all the week-end ; so I bagged them and set off. On my way I met a jobbing-gardener whom I knew. He had been for some straw at Ullock Farm to protect his potatoes from the frost. We fell into step together, and after we had gone a few yards, he said, looking at me searchingly : 'Ba goom, thoo hes failed a bit.' He was right. I had failed a bit, but I didn't tell him of my week-end.

That short bout of 'flu let me understand that we are all but little children weak. Since then, I have thought of it often, and wondered what would have happened to me, had I really taken pneumonia. And if it wasn't that incident which made me write this book while the going was good, then I don't know what it was.

This is a stormy, rainy evening. From my hut window I see the heavy clouds pass across the valley. Bassenthwaite Lake is grey. Often I have seen it blue and serene in the morning sunlight, and I have loved it. A gust of wind shook the hut just now. In the trees there is a moaning, and no birds sing. I have just poked my fire to a blaze ; it is the only friendly sight tonight. Soon I will make myself a cup of tea. That'll be even more friendly. Listen to the rain and wind ! Binnsey Fell and Bassenthwaite Lake are almost obscured by a grey veil, and sheets of rain are scudding across the Bogland. But I cannot finish this book on such a dreary note. Parting thoughts ought to be cheery ones. The last entry in my diary will make a happier ending :

In front of the hut the shadows are lengthening. It is the end of a gloriously lovely day. From my window I see the dark fingers halfway over the greensward of the glade. They will creep over imperceptibly to the path that goes down from the hut to the gateway by the road. Then they will rise up the dark, glossy Scots firs at the side of the path, until also they are in shadow. Across the warm valley they will go, past the murmuring Derwent, to climb at last the vast bulk of Skiddaw. For a glorious moment the twin peaks will be resplendent with mellow light, but they, too, will be overwhelmed by the advancing monotone. Only the strip of snow between the peaks will gleam, till night at last quenches even that stubborn whiteness.

But at the moment the sunset is very beautiful. I see only two rabbits grazing in the cool shadows up by the wood, but later, more will join them ; and as dusk falls, the glade will be full of those happy people.